HEARING MUSIC

The Art of *Active* Listening

by

Theodore M. Finney

NEW YORK

HARCOURT, BRACE AND COMPANY

11322

PRINTED IN THE UNITED STATES OF AMERICA
BY QUINN & BODEN COMPANY, INC., RAHWAY, N. J.

PREFACE

THIS book is the result of some years spent in the attempt to help more people to understand music. Its fundamental premises are that music is part of the cultural heritage of all and that it exists for an audience which, in the very nature of things, is made up of listeners who are not professionally trained musicians. The kind of help needed by a listener is quite different from a training for professional musicianship. Conversely, it can be asserted with some degree of truth that professional training does not necessarily produce an intelligent listener.

The present book is the result, then, of an attempt to present music to the listener so that he may understand it intelligently. Much that can be learned about music and musicians is of no concern to the listener as a part of the technic of his listening. This does not mean that any limit should be placed on the listener's curiosity about music. It does mean, however, that there is a vast difference between what he needs in order actually to hear music and what he might learn that has very little to do with his listening. It is not fair to the person whose interest has brought him to buy a book in which he expects to learn how to hear music, to spend time and energy reading about matters which have only slight bearing on what he wants to learn.

"Music is the universal language." This quotation, perhaps more often than any other, is used whenever the occasion seems to demand that something important be said about music. It is almost always used with the implication that the universality of music nullifies the necessity of learning music as a language. This implication is false. Music, in the sense that it is a language, must be *learned* just as any other language must be learned.

It is true that some individuals learn languages more easily than others; it is true, too, that most of us have forgotten how we learned enough of our mother tongue to use it for communication. But it must not be forgotten that we do learn even our mother tongue. We study it formally as long as we attend school, and most of us never master its use to the point where we are independent of such aids as the dictionary. The problem of learning is even more evident in connection with mastering a foreign language. The difficulties of grammar and syntax, to say nothing of the necessity for constant reference to a glossary, make the process of learning a new language a poignant illustration of the difficulties which the necessity for communication presents to the learner.

For the ordinary person who wishes to understand music, its language stands somewhere between the mother tongue and a foreign language. He has been conditioned to its sound because he has been hearing it most of his life. But he fails to comprehend much that he might hear because he has not learned to understand. The traveler abroad who does his shopping and eating only in the places which display the sign, *English Spoken Here,* has much in common with the person whose tired reaction to a symphony concert is: "Never again." Both result from failure to have learned to understand a language.

Learning to hear music has much in common with the learning of a verbal language. No one would expect to learn

Russian by reading about it in English. One cannot learn music unless he is brought into actual active contact with music. This book tries to encourage and direct the active contact which the listener makes with music. The beginner must make progress in learning the language: he must himself feel that he is getting on terms of better understanding with music. It has been the author's experience with students, whose number now runs to several thousand, that the method which this book develops will produce that effect.

Any book, however, can provide only a part of the method. The beginner must be given opportunity for repeated hearings of the music, until he can use the book as an aid in following the music with his mind. To that end records, phonographs, radio programs and concerts cannot be heard too often. In fact, records and phonographs should be used enough to wear them out. A collection of recordings, like any other library, is useful only when it is being used!

Several details of the method for listening which this book presents call for a prefatory explanation. First, the book would be useless without a copious citation of musical examples. Such examples have been given in normal musical notation, not because the author believes that a musician's ability to read music is a prerequisite to listening, but because he knows that the ability to follow the pattern of notation when someone else is playing is very easy to acquire. The examples, then, are not meant to be read as a musician reads music, but to be followed as the music is being played. By using them in this manner, the student will find that after he has once connected the actual sound of the music with its notation, he will have little difficulty in using the notated examples for purposes of review.

Second, the acquisition of the ability to hear how sounds

behave in a musical fabric has been made a prerequisite to any discussion of the meaning involved in music. It cannot be said too often that *musical meaning grows out of what the tones do.* It is equally true that the inexperienced listener is unable to perceive all that tones do. Until that perception has been cultivated it seems futile to attempt to form valid judgments as to what music means. One might as well expect to comprehend a foreign language because he has heard it spoken. The method here is first to develop listening independence. When the beginner has mastered that, he will be well on his way to knowing what music means. Until he has mastered it, no amount of telling will convince him.

Finally, every attempt has been made to describe what the listener hears in terms which can be understood by the listener who has no technical background. It is a mistake to make the beginner feel that his ignorance of the technical vocabulary of music is a handicap. As his interest develops he can easily manage the rather simple concepts which are new to him. The listener whose growing ability to hear music arouses his interest in technical matters will find the answers to many of his questions in the *Appendix.* Such material has been placed in an appendix rather than in an early chapter because the author is convinced that it is a stumbling block rather than a necessary aid to listening unless the beginner approaches it out of his own curiosity.

THEODORE M. FINNEY

ACKNOWLEDGMENTS

THIS book has not been finished without help from various sources. The following acknowledgments are due:

A quotation from *Kamongo* by Homer W. Smith, copyright 1932 by Homer W. Smith. By permission of the Viking Press, Inc., New York.

A quotation from a paper on "The Relation of Emotion to Musical Value" by Carroll C. Pratt, in the MTNA *Volume of Proceedings* for 1938, by permission of Carroll C. Pratt.

The translation by John P. Jackson of Nicholas Lenau's "Don Juan," by permission of J. B. Lippincott Co., New York.

Parts of the translation by Frederick Jameson of the text of Wagner's *Die Walküre,* by permission of G. Schirmer, Inc., New York, and Schott, Mainz.

Prof. Dayton C. Miller provided me with photographs of sound waves as part of the illustrative material for the chapter on tone-color. His interest in anything that touches the science of sound has earned the gratitude of all musicians who know him.

To the students in music appreciation classes at Carleton College, the Smith College Summer School of Music, and the University of Pittsburgh, the author owes a debt of gratitude for their patience in teaching him how to teach them. If, working together, we have come to a finer understanding of great music, our efforts have not been misspent.

The work of writing has been lightened by the help of Betty Cerra and Leonora Molinari, whose interest in the preparation of the manuscript deserves the author's gratitude. Finally, the author must make the admission that he cannot adequately express his gratitude to Molly for her constant encouragement.

T. M. F.

CONTENTS

Preface

Part One

THE LISTENER'S TECHNIC

Chapter 1

THE COMPOSER'S MATERIALS

THIS book has for its subject what is commonly called the appreciation of music. It will ask the reader to learn how to listen to music; it will suggest to many who have been listening all their lives that there is a better way to listen. This change can be made only with the consent of the reader; what the book contemplates doing and what its methods are to be should be perfectly clear at the outset.

For such clarification there can be no better starting point than an examination of the word which implies the changes we wish to make, the word "appreciation." Appreciation suggests to many musicians a type of popularization almost as distasteful as attempts at scientific popularization have been to some scientists. What does the word really mean? How may its true meaning dignify the inquiry upon which we embark and at the same time furnish the method for that inquiry?

Webster indicates several meanings for the verb "to appreciate." In one sense it means simply to rise in value. With this meaning it is not the listener but the music itself which appreciates: the music increases in value. There is a temptation to dwell upon this use of the word. It arises out of the impregnability of the wall which personal taste builds around the curiosity of many listeners. Jack London is said to have remarked that the words "I like" are the most important in the language. He might have said that the words "I don't like" have justified more barrenness than any other words in the language. If the whole process which leads to appreciation could begin with the objectivity inherent in this meaning of the word, if only we could stand aside with our undeveloped and incurious likes and dislikes and watch the *music* increase in value, then perhaps the culmination might be reached without too much stumbling against "I don't like."

For music to increase in value, however, implies a listener. Music must increase in value to you. Here again Webster may be consulted with profit. The definitions which apply are as follows: "To be critically and emotionally sensitive to the esthetic values of; to feel a warmth of satisfaction and approval in regard to." The first of these meanings, as applied to music, emphasizes values inherent in the music itself; the second stresses the "I like" relationship between the music and the listener. When these are put together we are justified in using them to chart our course. We are beginning a process which aims to *increase the value of music to you*.

Two questions arise from this preliminary discussion: What are those values and what can I do that they may increase for me? No one who has had much experience either with music or with listeners to music could have the temerity to suggest that those two questions can be answered completely and finally. It will take the rest of this book to start the reader on the road to finding his own partial answers. But some hints as to how those questions might be answered are not out of place.

"What are the values inherent in music?" is a question no one has answered to anyone else's complete satisfaction, but the way to an answer which will direct us into our work may be found by asking another question: "Why do people compose music?" All sorts of people have composed music and do compose music now, just as all sorts have written and do now write poems and plays and novels. It is often done at great expense of time and comfort. Why do they do it? They do it because they have something which must be said and for which music is the natural language. What that something is can be perceived, but seldom can it be restated through another medium of expression. The importance, for the composer, of what must be said, together with his ability to make himself articulate, is his measure, as men measure greatness and littleness. What a great composer, a great man who uses music as his language, finds worth saying should have value to the listener. Here are to be found, certainly, values which increase.

"What can I do that the values of music may increase for me?" The beginning of an answer to this question is to discover just how much music one really hears now. Music has been called a universal language. We have spoken of it as being a composer's language. Because "language" is so often used to indicate that music has something to say, and because the charm of this language has a universal appeal, it is easy to suppose that here, at last, is a tongue which needs no learning. The disappointments that follow attempts to approach music from this viewpoint, disappointments which every music lover has felt, prove this approach to be false.

There is a vast difference between the methods of spoken language and music. In a spoken language, generally, total meanings arise out of what we have come to agree that words themselves mean. In music, meanings arise out of what the sounds *do*. Music, in other words, means what the tones *do*.

Our first problem is to make sure that every sort of thing that tones can do is covered by our listening vocabulary. Is one listener, with his attention on the soaring tone of the violins, hearing what his neighbor hears, whose feet are tapping to the drums? Might not both learn to hear all of the music all of the time, and by so doing have approximately the musical experience which the composer wished them to have?

The reader might, with some justice, wonder why he is being asked to consider the materials of music as the composer's materials. It is only a matter of viewpoint. Musical materials are fundamentally the same whether they are viewed from the standpoint of composer, performer, or listener. The selection of a viewpoint is, however, important for a proper perspective of the route over which we hope to travel. Many listeners, in fact many people who undertake to train others to listen, insist that only as the listener can make some contact with music as a performer is a real understanding of music possible. That viewpoint is a tacit insistence that the materials of music are the performer's. Many arguments can be brought to bear against such a perspective. Chiefly, it overemphasizes the cult of great performers, which may be highly profitable for a time and for a limited few, in box-office reckoning, but is essentially spurious and in the long run is clearly not valid.

The three-sided composer-performer-listener communication begins with the *composer,* and it is only the fear that some impenetrable magic surrounds his work, a fear which perhaps we inherit from the Middle Ages with their guild secrets, that makes it difficult for us to begin to understand what he does. The composer himself knows what he is doing when he makes music. He has never asked for an audience trained as composers or performers. And, although he has sometimes been at fault in seeking self-glorification by surrounding what he does with an aura of magic, he nevertheless knows that the best audience he can have, the best there can possibly be, is one made up of those who have learned how to listen. And he will trust most those listeners who begin by understanding the materials with which he himself works.

Composers are often spoken of as creative artists. The use of this adjective in connection with what a composer does is just only in the sense that it has become so common that the dictionaries have been forced to recognize it. But in no real sense does the composer create his actual materials. He resynthesizes materials which already are at hand, in much the same fashion that a carpenter works with wood. This analogy cannot be carried too far, but it contains an element of truth which is illuminating. Almost anyone can understand what a carpenter does, certainly enough to use the product of his labor; almost anyone, too, can understand, enough for profitable use, the product of a composer.

The composer controls and directs, for our use, the materials out of which he makes music. Those materials are simply the things that tones can do, the ways that tones can be made to behave, the various qualities that sounds can have in relation to each other. What, then, are the composer's materials, his basic tonal resources?

That question can be answered by anyone who has heard even the simplest sort of music.

Sounds may be produced in an almost endless variety of ways. Each musical instrument (and the human voice is an instrument) has its own quality of sound, its own charac-

teristic sonority which is a result of the way sound is produced by it. In much the same manner as a painter transfers
the colors of his palette to his picture, the composer selects
and combines for his composition the sonorities of the instruments at his disposal. He uses not colored pigments which
reflect different vibrations of light, but instruments which
produce differently constituted vibrations of sound. Several
words have been used to describe this tonal resource: timbre,
clang tint, tone-color. They are, for the purposes of the
listener, synonymous; but to avoid confusion we will use
the word "tone-color." All the sorts of sonority and all their
uses in tonal combinations constitute one great tonal resource
for the composer: *tone-color*.

Sounds succeed each other, as they move past the point of
the listener's consciousness at which they are perceived, at
varying rates of speed and in different patterns. The composer has at his command an infinite variety of such speeds
and patterns. Because music exists in time, not in space, and
because humans measure the passage of time by applying
patterns to it, music could not exist nor could it be understood without this most basic element of rhythm. *Rhythm*
is another of the composer's resources, a fundamental part of
his materials.

Perceiving forward motion of definite speed and pattern,
produced at a monotonous level as, for instance, by handclapping or by beating a drum, gives us a concept of rhythm
as a musical resource which can be and often is used effectively apart from any other musical materials. Whether
rhythm by itself can constitute music is a question which
need not trouble us here. The fact, however, that the question is ever raised indicates the fundamental quality of
rhythm and implies what will shortly be seen to be true, that

the motion and pattern of rhythm can hardly be separated from the rest of the materials which are available to a composer. Forward motion, which, when it remains absolutely horizontal, we recognize as being purely rhythmic, may be given a vertical motion in combination with the horizontal. A line of sound which moves up and down while going forward is *melody*, one of the most attractive of the materials out of which music is made.

While tone-color, rhythm, and melody are the oldest musical materials and are present in nearly all historic and exotic musical cultures, the distinctive quality of Western music has resulted quite largely from the high development of a fourth material—harmony. Harmony, the sounding together of several tones in vertical relationship, is not only one of the most important parts of the composer's language; but it has, as the understanding of its possibilities has developed, modified and made more exact the use of all the other parts of the musical language.

Tone-color, rhythm, melody, harmony—these are the composer's resources, the basic materials out of which he makes music. They are, in consequence, the things with which those who desire a real appreciation of music must have a "listening" acquaintance.

Chapter 2

TONE-COLOR

TO most listeners, one of the most agreeable parts of the musical experience is the reaction to the quality of sound. From an instrumental or vocal solo to the ensemble of a symphony or an opera a great deal of the charm for the listener arises out of the fact that his sense of hearing is being gratified. This gratification may often take the form of an experience in which the listener loses himself in a world of great tonal beauty, in which he himself seems to become a part of that beauty.

There can be little question that this quality of music has been the initial attraction for most listeners, and, for that matter, for most makers of music. The discovery that here, in the realm of sound, is a source of intense sense-gratification has been the point of departure for many music lovers. The discovery, too, that he himself can produce a gratifying tone with voice or instrument has started many a music maker on his career.

If sense-gratification, if having the ear tickled by beautiful sounds, were the end of musical experience instead of its beginning, there would be little point in our present discussion. Like the charm of a beautiful speaking voice used constantly but saying nothing, music could become intolerable if its initial attractiveness were its final end. Here, however, where music exerts its first charm on many listeners, is the place to begin our practice in learning to listen.

Each musical instrument has its own characteristic tone-color. The implications of such a statement are enormous, and were it not for the ability of the human ear to generalize on the basis of how the tone is produced, this aspect of music would be chaotic. We are aware that violinists, for instance, recognize immense variations in the quality of tone produced from different violins or even from one violin played by different violinists. But despite this fact we are able to generalize sufficiently to recognize a *violin* tone. This *violin* tone is characteristic of the highest-pitched stringed instrument played with a bow. Thus we are able to speak about the tone-color characteristic of any given kind of musical instrument even though we recognize that from one individual instrument to another and from one performance to another there will be an interesting variation in tone-color. But that variation will seldom, if ever, go beyond what we take to be characteristic of the instrument in question.

Tone-color depends, then, upon the method by which the tone is produced. This method varies from one kind of instrument to another. Basically, sound is the result of a vibration, an alternate compression and rarefaction of the air. The sounds of different instruments vary because different kinds of vibrations are produced. This whole subject need not trouble the listener—it belongs rather to the domain of the physicist. It is mentioned only to indicate that, with the use of devices like the stroboscope, the sound-wave patterns characteristic of various instruments can be seen. What has long been apparent to the ear can be measured with utmost exactness.

From the standpoint of the ordinary listener, the scientific aspect of tone-color, however interesting it is in itself, cannot be of much help to intelligent listening. We perceive tone-colors as the characteristic sonorities of various instruments and not as vibration patterns. Our interest here is simply to quicken our perception with regard to tone-color, to become

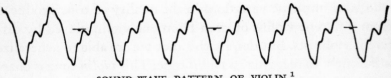

SOUND-WAVE PATTERN OF VIOLIN [1]

fully sensitive to one of the composer's important tonal resources.

The modern symphony orchestra has come into existence largely as a result of the search on the part of composers for constantly new, varied, and expressive tone-color. The color

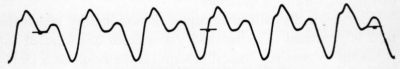

SOUND-WAVE PATTERN OF FLUTE

resources of the orchestra, with its kaleidoscopic possibilities, are almost without limit. At a moment, for instance, when the acoustics of the concert hall seemed to place a limit on what could be expected in the way of new tone-colors from an orchestra, the application of electrical amplification

[1] The smoothness of the line indicates absence of overtones. The tone of each instrument was photographed as the instrument produced middle C with medium loudness. Prof. Dayton C. Miller, of the Case School of Applied Science, Cleveland, Ohio, very kindly furnished the photographs.

and recording has opened an immense new territory for exploration.[2]

Because so much great music has been and is being written for the symphony orchestra, because opportunities to hear the orchestra either in concert hall, on phonograph records, on film sound tracks, or over the radio make its music increasingly available, and because the orchestra is the most complex musical medium, our study of tone-color may well begin with an attempt to master its intricacies.

We now begin to learn the language. We must learn to recognize, first by name, and finally as automatically as we recognize the meanings of words, the voices of the orchestra. The handiest names for those voices are the names of the instruments which produce them.

The instruments of the orchestra are normally divided into four groups: the woodwinds or reeds, the brasses, the percussion, and the strings. The musician accepts this grouping without quibbling, although he knows that the woodwinds include instruments no longer made of wood and that if he speaks of the group as reeds he must remember that the flute can be spoken of as one only because in its original form it was made from a large piece of reed.

When the composer writes for the orchestra he assigns the instruments to positions on his music paper, his score, in a conventional order which ranges them from top to bottom in sections:

[2] For the reader to whom this paragraph suggests an interesting field of exploration the author makes the following recommendations:
1. Read, unless by the time you see this footnote it has been superseded by a later work, *Toward a New Music* by Carlos Chavez.
2. Notice spots in recordings of standard works where amplification of single instruments has produced a tonal balance impossible in the concert hall.
3. Notice, in movie and radio, the "mixing" of music and sound effects—what might be called a tonal "moulage."

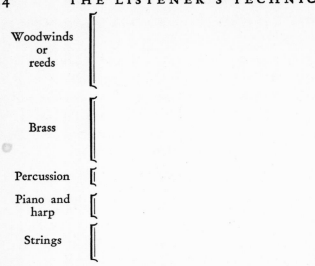

Woodwinds or reeds

Brass

Percussion

Piano and harp

Strings

Within each group he places the instrument which plays the highest part at the top, the lowest part at the bottom. Because many listeners, even those who have never seen an orchestral score, find, as they become interested, that following a score is fun, and because there is a definite logic in thinking about instruments as ranging from high to low, we will discuss them in the order in which they are placed on the composer's score.

ENGLISH	GERMAN	ITALIAN	FRENCH
Piccolo	Kleine Flöte	Flauto piccolo or ottavino	Petit flûte
Flute	Flöte	Flauto	Flûte
Oboe	Hoboe or Oboe	Oboe	Hautbois
English horn	Englisches Horn	Corno inglese	Cor anglais
Clarinet	Klarinette	Clarinetto	Clarinette
Bass clarinet	Bassklarinette	Clarinetto basso or clarone	Clarinette basse
Bassoon	Fagott	Fagotto	Basson
Contra bassoon or double bassoon	Doppelfagott	Contrafagotto	Contrebasson

ENGLISH	GERMAN	ITALIAN	FRENCH
French horn	Horn	Corno	Cor
Trumpet	Trompete	Tromba	Trompette
Trombone	Posaune	Trombone	Trombone
Tuba	Basstuba	Basso tuba	Tuba-basse
Kettledrums	Pauken	Timpani	Timbales
Bass drum	Grosse Trommel	Gran cassa	Grosse caisse
Side (snare) drum	Kleine Trommel	Tamburo militare	Tambour militaire
Cymbals	Becken	Piatti	Cymbales
Gong	Tam-tam	Tam-tam	Tam-tam
Triangle	Triangel	Triangolo	Triangle
Tambourine	Tamburin	Tamburino	Tambour de basque
Piano	Klavier	Pianoforte	Piano
Harp	Harfe	Arpa	Harpe
Violin { I / II	Violine (Geige)	Violino	Violon
Viola	Bratsche	Viola	Alto
Violoncello	Violoncell	Violoncello	Violoncello
Bass viol (contra bass, double bass)	Kontra Bass	Contrabasso	Contrebasse

Before attempting a description of the instruments of the orchestra which can be in any way valuable to the listener it must be made perfectly clear that a verbal description of tone-qualities is impossible. No one can learn to recognize the characteristic tone of a musical instrument by reading about it. Such discussion as follows must be used merely as a help in listening. Any attempt to correlate tone-color with actual color is fatal. The desire to describe the tone-color of instruments by using adjectives which denote emotional qualities is also dangerous. The word mournful, for instance, is occasionally applied to the tone-color of the English horn. Such typing is much more binding on the listener after he has made it than it is on the composer. Consequently it may lead to false listening.

WOODWINDS OR REEDS

The highest voice in the woodwind section is that of the piccolo. It is actually a small flute and is played like a flute. Its piercing tone-color may be heard above a considerable body of sound. Even in the best orchestras, with the best players, the piccolo is heard slightly out of tune often enough to lead one to suspect that part of the characteristic quality of its sound is the shrillness that results from a slightly faulty intonation. Another characteristic of the piccolo is its ability to play very rapid passages.

Several flutes are called for in most works for symphony orchestra. The instrument has a clear singing tone-color which may be quite loud in its highest register but which usually can be heard only against a rather subdued background. This is especially true when the flute is playing in its low register.[3]

The tone-color of both piccolo and flute is ordinarily described as clear and pure. This quality is due to the relative absence of overtones. Sound is produced in these instruments in the same way that a child makes a tone by blowing across the top of a bottle or a piece of pipe. The current of air from the mouth strikes the column of air enclosed within the bottle and sets it into vibration. The absence of any vibrating body other than air results in a relatively pure tone.

In the woodwind instruments other than piccolo and flute, the sound is initiated by a thin strip of reed which is set in vibration by the air from the player's mouth. In all reed

[3] For a description of other flutes less commonly heard in the symphony orchestra see an article entitled "Modern Alto, Tenor, and Bass Flutes" by Dayton C. Miller in the Music Teachers National Association *Volume of Proceedings* for 1938.

instruments the production of sound is controlled by the pressure of the player's lips on the reed as he blows air through it.

The oboe, which has a double reed, is the voice directly below the flute in the woodwind group. Its tone-color, due to the presence of many overtones, is slightly nasal but altogether rich and delightful. Although the oboe tone-color is by no means heavy or powerful, its unique quality makes it cut through the sound of the surrounding orchestra. For this reason it is often heard as a solo voice in the orchestra.

The English horn is probably no more English than the French horn is French. There is every reason to believe that its present name is due to a misunderstanding or mistranslation of the French word *anglé,* used to describe the shape of the pipe by which the reed is connected to the body of the instrument. Like the oboe, the English horn has a double reed; it is larger, lower-pitched, and characteristically slower-spoken than the former. Much of its range overlaps that of the oboe, and it is sometimes hard to distinguish its tone-color from that of its smaller relative. There is, however, a real difference between the two instruments which will be easily apparent to the ear that has become sensitive through careful listening.

The clarinet is placed below the English horn, or, if no English horn is used, below the oboe, on the composer's score. This indicates that it is considered as a lower voice. It has, however, a wider range than any other woodwind instrument and can play not only lower but higher than the oboe. The clarinet is sounded by a single flat strip of reed, held against the player's lower lip. Because of the type of reed, but even more because of the peculiar acoustics of the cylindrical bore of the instrument, the tone-color of the clarinet changes considerably from its lowest range to its highest.

The very name of the clarinet gives a clue to what was originally expected of it in the way of tone-color. The small, shrill, high-pitched trumpet common during and before the time of Bach and Handel (before 1750) was called *clarino* or clarion. As the early single-reed instrument which was the ancestor of the present clarinet gradually attracted attention, its tone-color was found quite similar to that of the *clarino;* and it had the added advantage of greater flexibility. In due time it was called the little clarion or clarinet and found its place in the symphony orchestra.

The modern clarinet no longer reminds us of an instrument we seldom hear, even though its upper compass has a slightly trumpetlike quality. It moves so smoothly and so rapidly and covers such a wide range with apparent ease that it is easy to distinguish. In its low register, especially when it is played softly, it has a somber, almost hollow sound which makes it one of the most valued instruments.

The bass clarinet is one of the very low voices of the orchestra. Its tone-color is similar in quality to the lowest register of the clarinet. It speaks slowly and its characteristic utterance can be picked out only when the rest of the orchestra is subdued.

The bassoon has a double reed, like the oboe and English horn, and consequently its tone-color has some of the same quality as those instruments. Conventionally it is used as the bass of the woodwind section, but it has such a distinct character of its own that it is often given solo passages. The peculiarly dry, rather wooden, nasal utterance of the bassoon can become, in the right tonal surroundings, surprisingly warm and interesting. And although it speaks rather slowly, it can cut through the sound of the rest of the orchestra quite incisively.

The double bassoon, or contra bassoon, is the low bass of the woodwinds, and is actually the lowest voice of the orchestra. Its tone-color is similar to that of the bassoon, but much heavier, and it is slower-speaking. Like the bass clarinet, it is difficult to manage and can be heard as a characteristic voice only when the composer takes pains not to blanket it with too large a body of sound.

The saxophones constitute a whole group of reed instruments which have not found wide use in the symphony orchestra partly because they overlap in range all the other reed instruments. They have a smooth and pleasing tone-color and are indispensable for concert bands and dance orchestras.

BRASSES

The French horn is not really the highest voice of the brass section, but its part is written directly beneath the woodwinds on a composer's score because of an old usage which has not completely disappeared. In many old scores it is the only brass instrument represented; it was used partly because composers felt that its quality would help to blend the woodwinds with the rest of the orchestra. Really it was treated as one of the woodwinds. This is still the case in much writing for orchestra, and the conventional chamber music group, the woodwind quintet, is composed of flute, oboe, clarinet, French horn, and bassoon.

What makes it desirable to use the French horn with woodwinds is a great richness of tone-color which seems to reach out and enclose and thus blend together the stronger individualities of the reeds. As one hears the French horn in an orchestra its sound seems to come from all directions; in fact, the player keeps the bell of his instrument turned away from the audience except when great volume is wanted.

As a solo instrument, the French horn is one of the most pleasing and altogether delightful voices of the orchestra. It has a wide range from a rather gruff low to a pervadingly rich high. Played softly, its round, liquid quality can be imitated by no other instrument. Played loudly, it has the power of a true brass and can at times be made to give out a percussive, almost explosive ring of great intensity.

The trumpet is one of the most familiar instruments of the orchestra, partly because of its extensive use in dance bands. It must not be confused with the cornet, which resembles it, but whose use is confined almost altogether to the military and concert band. The trumpet is the highest voice of the brass section. Its tone-color is brilliant, penetrating, and somewhat nasal. It is used frequently, especially in modern scores, as a melodic instrument, although for its traditional use as a "power" instrument in producing dynamic climaxes it has no substitute.

The use of the trumpet in music which is familiar to most listeners varies considerably. The reason is to be found in the changes which have been made in the instrument within little more than the last century. The trumpets of the late eighteenth century—the time of Haydn and Mozart and Beethoven—lacked valves and were hardly more than bugles. It was impossible to play a scale on them, and if the bugle-like series of tones which could be produced on any given trumpet did not fit the key of the music, the player had to change trumpets. Because of this inflexibility the instrument had a restricted use which can be traced very clearly in the orchestral music of the time. In the symphonies of Beethoven, for example, the discriminating listener can find many passages where the composer must have wished for a more flexible trumpet; not having one, he was forced to write parts which seem unnecessarily simple and at times rather harsh to the listener who knows the possibilities of the modern trumpet.

With the addition of valves to the trumpet all the possible tones within its range could be played without changing instruments. The trumpet became a much more vivid part of the orchestra, and composers were not slower than performers in exploring its new possibilities. Modern orchestral works, in consequence, make an increasingly varied use of the trumpet. It should be added, too, that the use to which the trumpet has been put in the modern dance band, especially in America, has added immensely to what may be expected from it in the way of flexibility.

The trombone is the tenor of the brass section, with a tone-color rich and smooth. Its dynamic possibilities range from a soft warmth to a volume of tremendous power. Because of its slide mechanism the trombone has possibilities possessed by no other brass instrument. These possibilities are utilized more often in dance bands than in symphony orchestras, but it is interesting to note that the tremendous technical achievements of trombone players in modern dance bands have been reflected in the increased demands made upon the trombone by modern composers of symphonic music.

The bass trombone is similar in tone to the ordinary trombone except that it has a lower range.

The tuba is the true bass of the brass section. Normally it speaks rather slowly, but it can produce a sound of great power and density. Seldom heard as a solo instrument, except in instances like Wagner's use of special tubas, its tone-color is indispensable to the total orchestral sound.

PERCUSSION

The cornerstone of the percussion section of the symphony orchestra is the set of kettledrums or timpani. The kettle-drums must be tuned to the tones indicated by the composer at the beginning of a score. They are played with two soft-headed sticks. As the key of the music changes—in older music, from movement to movement within a symphony; in newer music, often within movements—the kettledrums must be retuned. This is done either by turning the screws around the rim of the kettle or by a pedal mechanism. In music where rapid changes of pitch are necessary, the per-former must have either a pedal kettledrum or more than two of the sort tuned by screws.

The kettledrums are often heard in solo passages and are easily recognized by the fact that their sound has pitch. In older music they are almost invariably tuned to *do* and *sol* of the particular key and are used at points where the com-poser wishes to insist to the listener that he has now brought the music around to the home key. They furnish, moreover, one of the normal means of adding to the volume of orches-tral sound.

The "boom" of the bass drum, played normally with one stick, is too familiar to demand discussion. It is an active noisemaker and is used oftenest to accent the rhythm.

The snare or side drum is a military instrument, indis-pensable in the symphony orchestra because of its ability to mark rhythms. It is played by means of two wooden drum-sticks, either with the snares, which are cords stretched tight across the back head, so that the tone-color has the familiar rattle, or without the snares, when its tone-color approaches that of the tom-tom. Few listeners are entirely conscious of the immensely varied and intricate rhythmic patterns which are possible to the snare drum.

The cymbals are usually used in pairs and struck together. Their tone-color is often used to give a cutting edge to loud climaxes. At times, also, composers ask that the cymbal be struck with various types of sticks. As with many other percussion instruments, the basic sound of which is fairly easy to recognize, the listener can hardly predict what use the composer's imagination will find for it.

The orchestral bells, sometimes called the glockenspiel; the tubular chimes; the celesta, basically a set of orchestral bells played from a pianolike keyboard; even the xylophone—are all percussion instruments which produce sounds of definite pitch. The triangle produces a high metallic sound of comparatively indefinite pitch.

Rattles of various kinds, tom-toms, castanets, the tambourine, gongs, wind machines—in fact, any noisemaker for which the composer's imagination may discover a use—are regarded as members of the percussion section.

PIANO AND HARP

The piano has long been in use as a solo instrument accompanied by the orchestra, but as a member on a par with the others it has come into the symphony orchestra largely during the twentieth century. It might be mentioned in passing, however, that the instrument which the piano displaced during the eighteenth century, the harpsichord or clavicembalo, was widely used in the orchestras of its time.

As a constituent of the modern symphony orchestra the piano is often treated as a percussion instrument.

The harp needs little discussion from the standpoint of the listener. Its tone-color is unmistakable, whether it is used as an accompanying instrument in solo passages for other instruments or whether it contributes great, sweeping chords to the sound of the whole orchestra.

Piano and harp both have strings, but beyond this there is so little in common between them and the so-called string section that they are looked upon by composer and listener alike as belonging either in a separate section by themselves or in the percussion group.

THE STRINGS

The strings of the orchestra are the instruments which are normally played with a bow and which change their pitch as the result of stopping; that is, pressing down a finger to change the length of string that vibrates. The strings *make* the modern symphony orchestra. The characteristic tone-color of a large group of violins, violas, violoncellos, and basses is the backbone of the body of orchestral sound; without it the orchestra becomes what we in America call a band. When the possibilities of this tone-color began to be exploited fully during the eighteenth century, the modern orchestra came into existence.

Little space need be given to a description of instruments which are as familiar as the strings. The violins play a divided soprano part: first violins—second violins. The variety of tone-color possible is so great that composers have not yet exhausted it. The violas—slightly larger, lower in pitch, and with a somewhat nasal but amazingly rich tone-color—are the altos of the string section. The violoncellos, which, in the hands of modern performers, have a flexibility of utterance comparable to that of the violins, are the tenors of the string choir. The double basses, or bass viols, are the lowest-pitched instruments of the string section. They furnish the chief bass voice of the orchestra.

While the strings are used primarily as the most important voice of the orchestra—a sort of backdrop against which the other tone-colors of the orchestra may be displayed—each tone-color in the string choir may be utilized separately. Thus the chief player of each section of the stringed instruments is not only its leader, but also a soloist who may be called on for an individual contribution of tone-color.

Until recently such a discussion of tone-color would have furnished a fairly complete basis upon which the listener might build his own experience. But within the last few years a new element has removed some of the boundaries which formerly confined the possibilities of tone-color. That element is the electrical reproduction of sound.

How instrumental tone-colors could be combined has been controlled traditionally by the acoustics of the concert hall. The composer might hope that his music would be played always under ideal acoustic conditions, but in weighing the mass of sound represented by the notes he put on his score he had to remember the acoustics of the actual or possible concert hall. Therefore many tonal combinations were dangerous or impossible, and many failures by composers who were not always practical in this regard might be recounted. Thus one could hardly use the flute as a solo instrument in its low register and at the same time have the strings and brass playing with full volume of tone. Nor could the quality characteristic of an instrument playing softly be retained when that same instrument was asked to play loud.

Although we still hear much of our music under concert-hall conditions, it is no longer necessary that recorded or broadcast music be performed under them. As those who have charge of recording and broadcasting and those who compose for recording and broadcasting—it must be remembered that all moving-picture music is recorded—become more and more aware of the possibilities of the new conditions, we may expect tone-color resources to be tremendously enlarged. The careful listener to recordings, while he may discover many points at which the traditional concert-hall approach has almost ruined the performance, will also find considerable pleasure in discovering that the meaning even of well-known scores has been clarified by the possibilities of microphone placing and of "mixing."

The problem of mixing, for purposes of recording and broadcasting, is the old problem of the orchestral conductor under new conditions. From the standpoint of the intelligent listener the conductor has one, and only one, function. He must see to it that the music *sounds*. Making the music sound implies more than a faithful presentation of the tone-color of the music, but it does not include the kind of showmanship which distracts the listener's attention from his *hearing*. Music must be heard, not seen, and a so-called colorful performance of a conductor for the sake of impressing an audience is intolerable. The conductor's motions should be a guide for the musicians of the orchestra; beyond this they simply distract attention from the music. The listener should guard against mistaking the colorfulness of a performer for the tone-color of the music.

Mastering the technic of hearing tone-color is an exercise

that, not only because of its complexity, but because of the enlarged boundaries of tone-color which are now being exploited, will give the listener lifelong pleasure.

Practice that will make the listener sensitive to tone-color takes time. Fortunately, he can be getting it every time he listens to music. The orchestra presents the biggest problem, which we may attempt to solve in the following way:

First, become familiar with the tone-color of each instrument separately. The pair of records issued by RCA Victor called *The Instruments of the Orchestra* can be used for help.

Second, hear and learn the tone-color of each instrument against the background of other instruments. The four albums issued by Decca called *The String Family*, *The Woodwind Family*, *The Brass Family*, and *The Percussion Family* are excellent for this purpose. The pictures of instruments in each album may be of help. Remind yourself, when you are listening, that you are going part-way to meet the music: you are concentrating on learning to recognize a quality of sound.

Third, take any fairly complex piece of orchestral music and, as you listen to it, tell yourself what instrument or group of instruments, one after the other, has the center of your attention. On the chart at the end of this chapter, point, as you listen, to the name of the instrument you are hearing. A good many pieces might be recommended for this purpose. The "Scheherazade" Suite by Rimsky-Korsakov might have been composed for this very purpose. By the time you have heard it through, you will have heard every important instrument play the sort of music to which it is best adapted.

Fourth, make the acquaintance of famous passages in orchestral literature for each instrument. Nearly all of them have been given solos within important pieces of music. For instance, one can hardly think of the English horn without being reminded of the slow movements of Franck's Symphony in D minor and Dvorak's symphony "From the New World," or the prelude to the third act of Wagner's *Tristan and Isolda*. A list at the end of this chapter will help the listener to locate what he needs.

Finally, most listeners know more about the tone-color of instruments than they are aware. Don't spend too much effort on the ones you know. Work at those that are unfamiliar. And if you can't master the fine points of this kind of recognition without too much self-torture, let it go. An infallible or absolute tone-color recognition may be like absolute pitch recognition, a gift of nature. Some are able to recognize and name the pitch of any musical sound they hear. Either you can do that or you can't. But nearly everyone can learn *relative* pitch recognition; given a starting point, he can sing a tune. In like manner, every normal listener should be able to acquire a good degree of mastery of *relative* tone-color recognition.

Point at this chart as you listen.

STRINGS	WOODWINDS	BRASS	PERCUSSION
violin	piccolo	trumpet	kettledrums
viola	flute	French horn	bass drums
violoncello	oboe	trombone	snare drums
bass viol	English horn	tuba	cymbals
piano	clarinet		bells
harp	bass clarinet		gong
	bassoon		triangle
	contra bassoon		castanets
	saxophone		tambourine

RECORDINGS

The Instruments of the Orchestra Victor 20522, 20523
The String Family   Decca Album 90
The Woodwind Family   Decca Album 91
The Brass Family   Decca Album 92
The Percussion Family   Decca Album 93

Rimsky-Korsakov	"Scheherazade" Suite	Victor M-269
Franck	Symphony in D minor	Victor M-300
Dvorak	Symphony No. 5, "From the New World"	Victor M-273
Wagner	*Tristan and Isolda,* prelude to Act III	Columbia Set 101 Side 32

NOTE: The lists following give music in which each instrument is used for its characteristic tone-color.

WOODWINDS

Piccolo	Sousa	"Stars and Stripes Forever"
	Tchaikovsky	Symphony No. 4, Scherzo
	Tchaikovsky	"Nutcracker" Suite: "Chinese Dance"
Flute	Mendelssohn	*Midsummer Night's Dream:* Overture; Scherzo
	Tchaikovsky	"Nutcracker" Suite: "Dance of the Flutes"
Oboe	Schubert	Symphony No. 7 in C major: Andante con moto
English horn	Dvorak	Symphony No. 5 in E minor, "From the New World": Largo
	Franck	Symphony in D minor: *Allegretto*
Clarinet	Tchaikovsky	Symphony No. 5 in E minor: Andante of first movement, for low register
	Weber	*Der Freischütz:* Overture
Bass clarinet	Tchaikovsky	"Nutcracker" Suite: "Dance of the Sugar-Plum Fairy"
Bassoon	Tchaikovsky	Symphony No. 5 in E minor: Valse
	Taylor	"Through the Looking Glass" Suite: "Jabberwocky"

| Contra bassoon | Dukas | "The Sorcerer's Apprentice" |
| Saxophone | Bizet | "L'Arlésienne" Suite No. 1 |

BRASS

French horn	Strauss	"The Merry Pranks of Till Eulenspiegel"
	Mendelssohn	*Midsummer Night's Dream:* Nocturne
Trumpet	Liszt	"Les Préludes"
	Harris	Third Symphony
Trombone	Chabrier	"España" Rhapsody
	Harris	Third Symphony
Tuba	Sibelius	"Finlandia"

PERCUSSION

Kettledrums	Wagner	*Götterdämmerung:* "Siegfried's Funeral Procession"
Bass drum	Tchaikovsky	"1812" Overture
Snare drum	Strauss	"The Merry Pranks of Till Eulenspiegel"
Cymbals	Wagner	*Lohengrin:* Prelude to Act III

STRINGS

Piano	Stravinsky	"Petroushka" Suite
Harp	Rimsky-Korsakov	"Scheherazade" Suite
Violin	Brahms	Concerto in D major for violin and orchestra
Viola	Ippolitov-Ivanov	"Caucasian Sketches": "In the Village"
Violoncello	Bruch	"Kol Nidrei" (with orchestra; also good for harp)
	Rossini	*William Tell:* Overture
Bass viol	Beethoven	Symphony No. 5 in C minor: Scherzo

Chapter 3

RHYTHM

EVERYONE has had experience with space. Width, thickness, and length are concepts which hardly require explanation. If it is pointed out that a work of art requires a fundamental kind of *space* for its existence, one thinks immediately of the space limitations of a picture or a statue or a building. Those limitations may be set by the practical use for which the picture or statue or building is designed, but the artist nevertheless works within that required space.

The composer is confined, in like manner, to a kind of space. He may use the word length in connection with his space, but what he really means is a length of *time*. His space, except for a kind of thickness which must be discussed in a different connection, is time. Music exists in time. Lately, time limitations imposed by film and disc have made composers more and more aware of the time framework within which they work. Roy Harris, for instance, when the recording of his "Symphony: 1933" was being prepared, was told that the back of the last disc was not needed for the symphony, and that he had four minutes and twenty seconds of time available for another piece. He composed, for this definite amount of time, a piece for flute and string quartet which he called simply "Four Minutes and Twenty Seconds."

For the listener the length of the time is not as important

31

as the way in which the composer makes his music move through it. This movement may be a complex matter, and for a complete musical experience the listener must cultivate an awareness of the complexities involved, since they often carry much of the meaning of the music.

The passage of time is measured, for the purposes of music, by two devices: the recurrence of alternating strong (accented) and weak (unaccented) pulses with more or less regularity, and the use of patterns which are imposed upon or grow out of the pulsation. These two things constitute rhythm.[1]

Fortunately for both the development and the understanding of music, rhythm is a part of the composer's material which makes a close and direct contact with the human nervous and muscular systems. The listener responds almost automatically to the forward movement, to the rhythm, of the music he is hearing. One of our most human characteristics is that we are creatures of rhythm. The recurrence of the things we do, like eating and sleeping and going to work, obeys a rhythm which has vast importance to the comfort of our lives. We walk with a rhythm which grows out of the fact that one leg invariably steps harder or farther than the other. We learn muscular co-ordinations, such, for instance, as are required for manipulating a typewriter, much better and quicker if we make them rhythmically. Our minds superimpose rhythmic patterns upon such recurring noises as the ticking of a clock or the clicking of the wheels of a train against the rails. All these things and many others which the reader may note for himself demonstrate how

[1] The subtleties over which some musicians are inclined to argue with regard to the differentiation between time (tempo) and rhythm have so little importance to the listener that they may be dismissed from this discussion.

closely and characteristically human is the need to measure forward motion. It is so fundamental that music could not exist without it. A recognition of it and a cultivation of our responses to its subtleties make clear the contributions of rhythm to the composer's meaning.

A musician conceives the basic recurrence of strong and weak pulsations in terms of measures, the length and kind of which he indicates by a time signature; he suggests the speed he desires by a conventional speed description or tempo, generally in Italian. These two things are very simple and can best be understood in the musician's own terms.

A measure is the distance between points of strongest normal pulsation. That distance is stated, even by the musician, in mathematical terms. Thus if every fourth pulsation is strongest, he uses the number 4 in the numerator of his time signature to indicate the length of the measure; if every third pulsation is the strongest he uses the number 3. Then he decides what kind of symbol he will use to represent one pulsation in terms of musical notation, and this he indicates with another number in the denominator. Any sort of note, a whole note, which is represented in the time signature by the figure 1, half (2), quarter (4), eighth (8), or sixteenth (16), may serve his purpose. If the accent recurs every four whole notes his time signature is $\frac{4}{1}$; every four half notes, $\frac{4}{2}$; every four quarter notes, $\frac{4}{4}$; every three quarter notes, $\frac{3}{4}$; every two quarter notes, $\frac{2}{4}$; every six eighth notes, $\frac{6}{8}$; and so on.

This is not too technical for the listener. The ordinary person who has no knowledge of physics and chemistry but who wants to do some photography for his own pleasure will have a great deal more trouble with the comparatively much more complex mathematics of the relationships of lens and film area, of light strength and emulsion speed. Yet he will soon master them.

Music can hardly be understood without the listener's responding to measure. The commonest measures come to his ears countless times. They are represented by the time signatures $\frac{2}{4}$, $\frac{3}{4}$, $\frac{4}{4}$, $\frac{4}{8}$, $\frac{4}{2}$, $\frac{6}{8}$, $\frac{9}{8}$, $\frac{12}{8}$. The listener will find that these simple measures often serve the composer as a framework for more complex and varying rhythms; he will find, too, that simple basic measures do not always suffice, and the composer may use more complex combinations such as $\frac{5}{4}$ and $\frac{7}{4}$.

The speed at which the measures are supposed to move is indicated in several ways. Commonest is a tradition which musicians have inherited from the time when Italian was their international language. Instead of directing that their music should be performed simply slow or fast or medium fast, musicians habitually use such Italian words and groups of words as appear on our concert programs—copied from the printed music—to indicate the speed of the parts of long works. Examples are: *allegro,* meaning brisk or lively; *andante,* moderately slow; *largo,* very slow. Verbal description of speed can give, at best, only a clue. For greater accuracy composers and editors often indicate the number of pulsations per minute, as ♩ = 90. Because speed is relative, as an automobile driver discovers when he tries to *feel* thirty miles an hour in a town after a long stretch at sixty in the open country, the whole matter of the speed of musical movement must be referred by the listener not to a verbal description or a mathematical formula but to his muscles. At best the composer's indication of speed will only suggest what his muscles may expect. Dancers and marchers have no difficulty in recognizing different speeds and variations of speed. No one would suggest dancing or marching in a concert hall in order to feel the speed of music; listeners are often seen, though, who cannot get the feel of a rhythm without moving their fingers or feet or heads to it. For the rare listener who has difficulty about sensing rhythm differences, no better practice can be suggested than that when he has the chance, by himself, he should let his muscles *go* with the music to which he is listening.

So much for the first aspect of time measurement involved in music. It is basic. If a composer were to try to make music without the fundamental patterns of rhythmic pulsation which are supplied by measure and speed, the listener would supply them from his own experience. When, for example, the horn of a parked car begins to sing for its own amusement because of an electrical failure, the worker in a near-by office begins to count and feel the passage of time rhythmically in the hope that he may be able to count the singing to an end. But these basic pulsations are only the foundation upon which the rhythmic structure of a piece of music is built. The structure itself grows out of the rhythmic patterns which the composer selects to characterize each individual piece of music.

Certain basic pulsations and speeds become, with only slight additions, the rhythmic patterns out of which musical structures develop. This is especially true of dances. The waltz pattern is only a slight alteration of the triple measure:

The fox trot is another example—with a fundamental duple measure:

Many other dances, however, take their character from a more complex pattern that is superimposed upon the basic pulsation. In the habañera, the most familiar example of which is to be found in Bizet's *Carmen,* the time signature is a simple $\frac{2}{4}$ but the dance is marked by a constantly reiterated pattern which in this case is heard in the accompaniment:

The composer may use other rhythms along with this, as he desires. Both the polonaise, familiar in many works of that name by Chopin, and the bolero, which to most modern listeners means specifically the orchestral piece by Ravel, have a $\frac{3}{4}$ measure as their basic pattern. Both, too, have the same superimposed rhythmic pattern, either or both of the following:

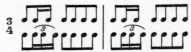

They differ chiefly in speed. As in the habañera, the composer may exercise his ingenuity in combining other rhythmic patterns with the basic one. The mazurka is another example. Known largely because of the attraction it had for Chopin, it is based on a fundamental triple rhythm, with the following rhythmic pattern:

The listener who is interested in dance rhythms will find an endless variety to keep his interest alive. The variety is infinite, so that it would be fruitless to attempt to make a complete catalogue. Our main purpose here is to cultivate a sensitivity to the qualities of the basic forward movement of all music. We must be alert, as we listen, to the patterns by which that forward movement becomes clear. That many, if not all, of those patterns have come to us from dance music is not surprising when it is remembered that the primary function of dance music is not only to accompany but to impel bodily movement.[2] But more important than the source of any rhythmic pattern is the way it is used by the composer in making music. This is of vast importance to the listener because listening consists basically in discerning and following patterns.

A rhythmic pattern is often imposed on a basic pulsation with which it conflicts. When this happens the accents of the basic pulsation are displaced and by that displacement made more prominent. The effect is called syncopation. It appears prominently in much dance music, even dance music not of twentieth-century America, and it is one of the favorite devices by which composers call attention to the significance of their rhythms.

Accents displaced:

Basic pulsation:

Rhythmic patterns may be thought of as coming to the ear all on one level, as they would be if they were sounded by a drum. But in most listening, rhythmic patterns which

[2] See Evelyn Porter, *Music Through the Dance*. Charles Scribner's Sons, 1938.

measure the forward motion of the music are combined with another kind of motion. They maintain their function as horizontal motion, but they take on, along with that horizontal motion, an undulating motion up and down which makes them fundamental not only to rhythm but to what in Chapter 1 we called melody.

RECORDINGS

Harris	"Symphony: 1933"	Columbia 68183-68186
	"Four Minutes and Twenty Seconds"	Columbia 68186
Bizet	*Carmen:* Habañera	Victor 1145
Chopin	Polonaise, Op. 26, No. 2	Victor 7391X
Ravel	Bolero	Columbia Set No. X22
Chopin	Mazurkas: Op. 33, No. 4	Columbia 7141-M
	Op. 63, No. 3	Victor 6879
	Op. 67, No. 4	Victor 6879

Chapter 4

MELODIC LINE

NEARLY everyone has had the experience, when looking out of the window of a fast-moving railway train, of having his eyes follow the line of telegraph wires strung on poles along the track. The constant dip and rise of the wires from one pole to the next, the rise and fall as the line of poles descends into a hollow or rises over a hill while the train moves along on a level track, exert an irresistible attraction. The eye is following a line; what it lacks in visual interest that line makes up in forward continuity and vertical rise and fall which fix the attention. Such a visual response gives us a clue to a similar aural response.

The ear follows, in almost exactly the same manner, a melodic line which has many similarities to the visual line of the telegraph wires. The aural response is perhaps not quite so automatic as the visual, but for that very reason it may arouse greater interest.

When we think about what we ordinarily call a tune or a melody, most of us have a preconceived set of requirements which the tune must meet before we will accept it as such. It must be tuneful, for instance, whatever that means— perhaps that it must be singable, or that it must lend itself to whistling, or that it must be easy to remember, or that we can try it on the piano. Whatever these personal requirements of a tune may be, they are often responsible for the failure of many listeners to find anything of interest in much of the music to which they are exposed when they attend concerts or listen to the radio.

Let us forget whatever concepts we individually have built up for tune and melody and return to the much more simple and equally more fundamental concept of melodic line. It is a line of sound, moving past and attracting the attention of the ear just as the telegraph wires attract the eye. Perhaps it disappears momentarily, as the wires do when the train goes through a cut or over a bridge; that very disappearance emphasizes the importance of the line and makes its reappearance an event.

With such a concept of melodic line and no other, no matter how strongly our individual tastes may try for the moment to dictate to us, we are ready to learn how to follow— to follow clear through from beginning to end—any piece of music we may hear. Our listening, as far as melodic line is concerned, is based too much on what we think a composer ought to make his music do, and not enough on an attempt to discover what the composer has really done.

How does a composer make a melodic line? There are almost as many answers to that question as there are examples of composers' work. The question is one that must be asked and answered for each piece. The question itself implies that the composer *makes* his melodic line, and this will surprise many listeners to whom all the processes of a composer's work are a kind of magic which can be left unexplained by calling it inspiration. Inspiration is involved, but the whole process of training to which composers subject themselves gives them a technic which helps them to *make*, besides other things, a melodic line. One of our most fruitful approaches to an understanding of music is to ask and to attempt to answer, for every piece of music we hear, this unavoidable question: *How did this composer make the melodic line for this piece?*

Answering this question will always be fun. At first it will have some of the same difficulties as learning the grammar and vocabulary of an unfamiliar language. The listener will have to look in the back of the book for some of the words. But eventually, as in any other learning process, the question will be answered with as little effort as it takes for the ordinary person to use his mother tongue.

Let us begin by answering the question for some specific pieces of music. A good starter is the familiar air, "La donna è mobile" ("Woman is fickle"), from Verdi's *Rigoletto*. This song has a melodic line which will fulfill almost anyone's demands of a tune. It has been called a barrel-organ piece by those who think it is a sign of superiority to show contempt for music which has the power to appeal to the barrel-organ man's customers. But anything subtler would have failed to serve the purpose which makes "La donna è mobile" so important dramatically in the opera.

Verdi had to have a piece of music which would unfailingly identify one of the characters after it had been sung only once. The Duke, with whom the song must be connected, is the intended victim of an assassination plot which, when it misfires, finds its victim in Gilda, the heroine. Gilda's father, Rigoletto, has instigated the plot; and as he is at last about to throw the sack containing the victim's body into the river, the Duke's song, "La donna è mobile," is wafted to him as the Duke wanders by on his way home. It has been heard only once before, but snatches of it now are enough to tell that Rigoletto's plot has gone wrong. That Verdi knew his piece would satisfy these requirements is demonstrated by the story related by Streatfeild in his *Masters of Italian Music:*

When the roles were distributed, the tenor who was to play the Duke found a blank in his part at the beginning of the third act. He went to Verdi and asked what it meant. "Don't be in a hurry," said the *maestro,* "there is plenty of time." Every day it was the same story; the tenor petitioned in vain for his missing song. At last, the day before the final rehearsal, Verdi gave him the manuscript of the famous "La donna è mobile" but not before he had made him promise not to sing or whistle a note of it to a living soul. At the rehearsal everyone was laid under a solemn oath not to divulge a note of the music before the performance. Verdi knew the quickness of Venetian ears. He knew that if the melody of the song were once heard outside the walls of the theater, it would be all over Venice in a few hours, and at the performance the gilt would be off the gingerbread.

How did Verdi *make* a melodic line that would so surely satisfy the dramatic and musical requirements of the opera?

First refresh your memory of the piece by playing it again.

The melodic line begins with a six-note group which immediately shows us how clearly a melodic line is related to the rhythmic pattern we discussed in the last chapter. This group of six tones, which we may call a *melodic motive,* gets its character partly from its rhythmic pattern.

This melodic motive is simple, direct, unforgettable. Out of it Verdi continues his song. First comes an instrumental introduction, with the motive used three and a half times.

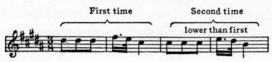

Next it is slightly changed in melodic contour, but without rhythmic alteration beyond adding an extra short note or grace note. The resemblance cannot be missed:

Then the first half of this form of the motive is repeated:

At this point we may revert to the analogy of the telegraph wires. If our view of them is briefly interrupted, we watch for them all the more eagerly. Verdi has us following the line of his melody, and by means of a break in the middle of the fourth repetition of the motive he provokes us into listening harder for what is to follow. What follows is more of the same motive, with the tenor singing:

After using his original motive eight times, Verdi repeats the music which the tenor has sung, making a melodic line which consists of twelve repetitions of the same motive. By that time, certainly, the listener can be expected to have it fairly well fixed in his mind. Verdi then introduces a new melodic motive, slightly more complex than the first:

This he uses three times, moving it upward each time, and changing the end of the third repetition:

(changed here)

Then, in view of the care which he has taken in sticking to his subject, Verdi becomes almost extravagant. After using his new motive only three times he introduces another so cleverly that it seems to come as a necessary result of the change he made in the third use of the one which it follows:

This, in turn, is followed by another, in the orchestra, while the tenor catches his breath in preparation for his long note and flourish:

But this motive returns us to its predecessor, and the two of them combined go along under the tenor's long note:

With a proper ending the labor of melody making is complete. The melodic line we have described is repeated in its entirety to finish the piece. After the song that we know as "La donna è mobile" is finished, however, the music of the opera continues with a long descending melodic line for the orchestra, made of twelve more repetitions of

NOTE: From here on, throughout the book, this staffless "skeleton" notation will be used where it is adequate to indicate materials which are already familiar.

How did Verdi make this melodic line? He invented these four short motives:

How he invented them and how he knew what to do with them are beyond this study. What he did with them is our affair, however, because an understanding of the process will make us more intelligent listeners. We might make a diagram:

Introduction . . . . singer	
Motive one	Motive one
four (three and one-half) times	eight times

singer . . . . orchestra . . singer . .				singer has long note ending in flourish orchestra
Motive two	Motive three	Motive four	Motive three	Motives three and four
three times	once	once	once	twice

Introductory passage again . . singer	
Motive one	Motive one
as before	as before

singer . . . . . . orchestra . . singer . . .				singer has long note ending in an extra flourish which tenors like to "jam" orchestra
Motive two	Motive three	Motive four	Motive three	Motives three and four
as before	as before	as before	as before	as before

This may seem a rather complex analysis for a very simple piece of music. Its difficulties will disappear if the listener follows the diagram a few times with his finger while listening to the music. The whole process of making a melodic line should seem so simple to the listener that he is tempted to make one himself. Perhaps he can; a good many people have.

This excursion into a complex analysis should have taught us several things:

First, a melodic line is made of motives.

Second, these motives combine the undulation of melody with the pattern of rhythm.

Third, once the melodic line is safely moving, new motives may be introduced with less necessity for their repetition.

Fourth, slight changes in both rhythmic pattern and melodic direction do not destroy the individuality of the motive.

Melodic motives may be long or short, simple or complex, easy to discern or hard to find, but they will be present in most of the music we hear. The only exception will be music so subordinated to a verbal text that the text claims most of the listener's attention, and the absence of a melodic motive in such a case as this only emphasizes the attention it must claim when it is present. The rhythmic pattern of a melodic motive, because of the very nature of our reaction to rhythm, will invariably be one of the identifying qualities of that motive. The tendency of a composer to add several new motives after the melodic line is well started is universal and should be a source of continual interest to the listener. Finally, the complexities of melodic line which trap and discourage many listeners invariably develop from subtle changes in the shape and character of melodic motives. One of the most fruitful sources of pleasure in listening is to

follow, in a melodic line, the increasing freedom with which
the composer unfolds and expands his melodic motives.

This is worth doing at least once in detail. It will also give
us experience with a more complex but fundamentally quite
simple melodic line. Let us examine an orchestral piece—one
which, on first hearing, will seem too complex for the sort
of analysis we made of Verdi's "La donna è mobile." The
opening Prelude of Wagner's *Tristan and Isolda* will serve
our purpose.

Wagner made the predominant melodic line of this Prelude from the following melodic motives:

The first time they are heard the second motive begins before the first ends, tone-color being used to keep their iden-
tities distinct. A clearer picture would be one like this:

And later, a third motive appears:

The subtleties of Wagner's use of these melodic motives un-
fold as follows: The Prelude begins with motive 1 stated by
the violoncellos, with motive 2 following immediately, played
by the oboe. This takes four measures. Then both motives
are played again, at a higher pitch—which was Verdi's procedure with his first motive—motive 2 being played this time

by the clarinet. So far we have heard a melodic line which may be charted like this:

Wagner next uses both motives again, returning to the tone-color of the oboe for motive 2. This statement also has been moved upward, so the process of raising the pitch has been continued. But in this third statement the motives begin another kind of expansion. Motive 1 begins at another point in the measure and is extended in length, so that it falls one step farther than it has before:

This is answered by a version of motive 2 which is also extended, rising higher than before:

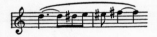

The careful listener will find in this third statement of these motives that Wagner is beginning to insist more and more upon the *direction of the motion* which characterizes each of them. Beneath this third appearance of motive 2 the English horn reinforces its upward motion in this way:

and the bassoons remind us of the downward motion of motive 1 by doing this:

In this third repetition, then, Wagner has given us a combination of melodic lines which include both motives:

Motive 2
upward motion of 2

Motive 1
downward motion of 1

Next, this combination of motives is moved up an octave and repeated. Then begins the process of motive subdivision so characteristic of the sort of thing the listener is continually being asked to follow and understand. The violins state very softly the essence of motive 2:

and this is answered, with increasing intensity, by the flutes, oboes, and clarinet. Then, over a tremendous chord, this upward motion is expanded, to introduce motive 3:

When motive 3 arrives, played by the violoncellos,

the listener will feel that it belongs; its first three notes are another way of saying what Wagner has discovered for us to be the essential element of motive 2. What is new is the wide melodic drop of the last part of motive 3.

As the melodic line of this Prelude develops, Wagner makes new combinations of every aspect of his motives which will serve his purpose. A measure-by-measure verbal analysis could hardly hold the reader's attention, but an attempt to hear and understand this melodic line will provide many hours of intensified musical experience, experience that will bring with it an enriched understanding not only of how music is made but of music itself. One thing this Prelude does not have in common with the Verdi song: it cannot be completely understood with a few hearings. This quality of much great music, a quality of holding back its complete charm while the listener grows into an acquaintance with it, is one of the most human qualities of this art. To say that an acquaintance grows on you is to compliment either a person or a piece of music.

Try to find, in this Wagner Prelude, the following: motive 3 broken in the middle, its parts recombined in reverse order, and followed by what we called the essence of motive 2:

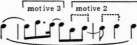

The rhythmic pattern of the first part of motive 3 given a new melodic shape and combined with the essence of motive 2:

Now where does this melodic figure come from?

Then the rhythmic pattern with which we are now familiar
is given a new melodic shape, introduced by a rapid rising
scale, and followed by another familiar motive segment.

Combinations like this appear:

One thing more must be said of the Wagner piece. This
method of *making* a melodic line is purely musical. But
Wagner was writing dramatic music, an introduction to a
drama which, when the Prelude is being heard in the theater,
is about to be performed on the stage. The melodic motives
which he uses, and some of their recombinations—such even
as the appearance, at the bottom of the music, of a group
of three tones which combine the rising inflection of motive 2 with the wide fall found in motive 3—

draw to themselves, from the context of their use in the
drama and from the very motion involved in their sound, a
psychological, dramatic significance which gives them another kind of meaning. In this relationship to the drama we
call them leading motives. Certainly, however, any value
and significance that this melodic line may have for the listener from Wagner's use of leading motives must wait upon
the listener's understanding of that same melodic line as a

musical entity growing out of the use of melodic motives. Leading motives as such are not our present interest.

In attempting to understand the melodic line of a piece of music which is new to the listener, the first step must be to find *and remember* the motives out of which that line is made. This is seldom difficult, especially for the listener who has gained some insight into how a composer works. The composer, if he wishes his music to be understood, must make it easy to listen to, which means that he must so present the motives that it will be difficult to miss them. A reexamination of the two pieces we have discussed will demonstrate the care with which both Verdi and Wagner presented their melodic motives. What the composer has taken so much care to present must be worth the listener's complete and intelligent attention.

Our interest so far has been devoted to only a part of the musical fabric. Very little music consists of only one melodic line, as the Wagner Prelude especially shows. Our attention must now turn to the task of hearing more than one melodic line at a time.

RECORDINGS

Verdi	*Rigoletto:* "La donna è mobile"	Victor 1704 (Gigli)
		Victor 1616 (Caruso)
Wagner	*Tristan and Isolda:* Prelude to Act I	Victor 6585

Chapter 5

SIMULTANEOUS MELODIC LINES

WE have had not only a glimpse at the process by which
melodic lines are made but some experience in following the thread of a single melodic line through a piece
of music. Our next interest must be an extension of the
ability to hear one melodic line so as to grasp the melodic
qualities of an entire musical fabric. Music is, in many of
its aspects, woven in a way which has many points of similarity with other fabrics. It is to the texture of this musical
fabric that we must turn in our next listening problem.

The texture of a piece like "La donna è mobile" presents
very little difficulty. The one thread which is the melodic
line dominates the fabric to such an extent that one hardly
notices the reiterated rhythmic and harmonic substructure.
That this substructure is a traditional and almost trite waltz
accompaniment does not serve to force it on our attention:

It gets started and runs along almost out of sight, a kind of warp over which the glittering thread of the melody is imposed. By itself it has virtually no melodic significance. Music of this type, where the single melodic line carries the whole melodic interest of the music, is called *monophonic* in texture. The listener will immediately recognize that most popular songs, ballads, folksongs, and a great deal of the music he hears in the concert hall belong to this category. The word which describes it is a good one to remember: *monophonic*.

Not all music, however, is monophonic in texture; what is more, much music that is predominantly monophonic has moments when the fabric becomes a web of melodic lines. This means that the listener must be prepared to follow a melodic texture which is *polyphonic*. The Wagner Prelude to *Tristan and Isolda* contains many passages which are polyphonic, where several melodic motives are woven together into a fabric and are to be heard simultaneously. A striking example of this procedure has already been illustrated:

Motive 2
Upward motion of 2

Motive 1
Downward motion of 1

The listener will be able to find many similar instances in the same piece of music.

Several kinds of polyphonic music are familiar to everyone. First on the list must come the round. The round has only one tune, but that tune furnishes the melodic material for a polyphonic fabric, as, for example, the well-known "Scotland's Burning":

Braided together, the polyphonic fabric looks like this:

Most of us are familiar with this type of polyphony, not as listeners but as performers. To keep to our own part, we have probably had to sing loud enough not to hear the other parts, for fear their pull would get us off. This is a problem for the listener too, but the pull of interest back and forth between different points in his intricate fabric is one of the composer's aims.

The round is a device for weaving together differently timed appearances of the same melodic line. Another polyphonic device with which most of us are familiar is that of weaving together two or more separate and distinct melodic lines. The classic example, which has been attempted in most schoolrooms and service club luncheons, is to sing "The Spanish Cavalier" and "My Name is Solomon Levi" at the same time. It usually ends in an uproar, but it can be done:

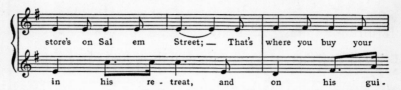

The round is one of the oldest devices for expanding music beyond a single unaccompanied melodic line. We have an example that was written down in England in the thirteenth century, the famous "Sumer is icumen in." Hardly any younger is the device of singing two or more distinct songs at the same time. It has always been a source of musical pleasure. The Bachs had a hilarious time at their family reunions, making up what they called a *quodlibet,* which is exactly what we have been describing.

More familiar than either of these devices, especially to our younger friends, is the polyphonic exercise known as the jam session. A music historian, if he has heard of the jam session, as most of them have, might perhaps wish to describe it as a polyphonic improvisation and might point out that this is something very old that was practiced by the church choirs of medieval Europe for several centuries, beginning somewhere between the time of Charlemagne and the Crusades. Still, lots of us know about polyphonic music at first hand through contemporary jam sessions. Those who are most familiar with this type of music are the first to suggest that its proper appreciation and understanding demand considerable study on the part of the listener. Mr. Wilder Hobson, in his book entitled *American Jazz Music,* has much that is of extreme interest to say on this subject. He has transcribed an improvisation of three choruses of the "Yellow Dog Blues" in which the improvised texture is clearly polyphonic.[1] In writing of this type of music, Mr. Hobson says: "Multilinear music of any sort seems to be less easily comprehended than music of a single melodic line with chordal support." With the blessing of even the jazz expert, then, we will go on to some exercises in listening to multilinear or polyphonic music.

The famous quartet from Verdi's *Rigoletto*, "Fairest daughter of love" ("Bella figlia dell'amore"), is an excellent piece with which to start. Verdi, with his unerring sense of what would succeed on the opera stage, has here written another piece that is so popular for its luscious sound that most listeners fail to perceive its more important excellences. Perhaps we, even, should play it once or twice before we study it in order to get our senses accustomed to its surface attraction.

Now, let's see what it really is. First, with a most unobtrusive orchestral accompaniment, it is a song for four voices: in the order of their entrance, tenor, contralto, soprano, baritone. Dramatically, it is one of the high points of the opera. This drama we must understand, and we can do it best by telling part of the story and drawing a diagram. The actors are:

The tenor. The Duke, who a few moments before has been singing "La donna è mobile" as a kind of prelude to the kind of entertainment he hopes the evening will produce.

The contralto. Maddalena, the girl with whom the Duke is momentarily enamored.

The soprano. Gilda, the court jester's daughter, who is in love with the Duke and who is heartbroken as she discovers that he is unfaithful.

[1] Wilder Hobson, *American Jazz Music*, p. 67.

The baritone. Rigoletto, Gilda's father, who seeks vengeance for the Duke's mistreatment of his daughter.

The action takes place at a lonely house in the country. The Duke and Maddalena are inside; outside, Rigoletto has brought Gilda to prove to her the Duke's unfaithfulness. Four emotions are thus present dramatically. The Duke is enjoying his lovemaking. Maddalena is coyly exercising her technic of keeping the Duke interested. Gilda is stunned by this proof of the Duke's unfaithfulness. Rigoletto is trying to comfort Gilda and at the same time is talking about revenge. Four people could hardly make an understandable *verbal* polyphony of this sort of situation. Without music, the situation would have to be conveyed in some different manner. But the music, when it is heard as a fabric of distinct lines, gives us not only a fascinating texture of sound but a counterpoint[2] of emotions. Four emotions, then, can be heard simultaneously; the words are comparatively unimportant in conveying them. Verdi's success with this piece makes it such a *tour de force* that we willingly accept the stretch of probabilities by which the Duke and Maddalena, who are unaware that the other two members of the quartet are in the neighborhood, unite with them so euphoniously.

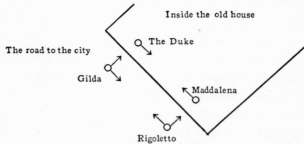

Inside the old house

The road to the city

The Duke

Gilda

Maddalena

Rigoletto

[2] A technical word which could hardly be avoided at this point. It refers to the process of weaving melodic lines together and is simply a shortened translation of the Latin phrase, *punctum contra punctum,* which means note against note.

The Duke begins with a phrase characterized by the motive
of its first three notes:

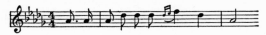

This becomes the familiar tune of the quartet:

Maddalena talks rapidly, with a melodic motive which fits
her character:

Gilda is given a drooping phrase which, in the way it falls
away, characterizes her part in the situation:

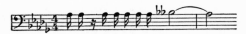

Rigoletto enters with the strength of the down beat in his
favor, but the rapid movement of his part keeps out of the
way of the movement of the other parts:

Verdi is careful to let the listener hear the entrance of each
part clearly; the character of each melodic line, together with
the tone-color of each voice, makes the task of following
the four lines not too difficult. When all four parts are moving, the fabric becomes a glittering musical brocade, and the
listener's attention is drawn back and forth from one thread
to another. The listener will have mastered its intricacies and
will have made considerable progress in listening to this sort
of music if, at the final note of the piece, he finds himself
to have been so attentive to the music that he feels the re-

lease of his attention. Good listening can hardly be passive.
Try it!

The pleasure of mastering the ability to hear music of
polyphonic texture leads the listener inevitably to the music
of J. S. Bach. Here, beyond all argument, is a great composer whose music demands the ability to follow the melodic
lines interwoven into one fabric. Bach's music makes other
demands on the listener too, but we can easily select a piece
which will serve our present purpose. Let us take the second
movement of the Concerto in D minor for two violins.

The tone-color interest of this movement, as of the whole
concerto, consists in the sound of two violins against a body
of accompanying strings. The most important melodic lines
appear in the solo parts, but it would be a mistake not to
direct some of our listening attention to the accompanying
parts. Here, as in all other listening, the first thing is to discover the motives out of which the melodic lines develop.

The music begins with two motives played simultaneously.
The more important is given to the second solo violin:

This grows immediately into one of the melodic subjects of
the piece:

Sounding with this melodic line is another at the bottom of
the score, one which will continue with hardly a break until
the final note:

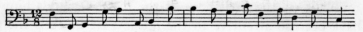

When the second solo violin reaches the end of its two-measure subject the first solo violin answers in a higher register with a line constructed from the same motive; thus the listener hears this motive first in one melodic line and then in another. At this answering entrance the second solo violin takes up another, more rapid motive:

From these three motives, then, Bach makes his melodic lines. The listener will find in unraveling the texture of the piece that any one of the three will be heard at the top, in the middle, or at the bottom of the music, that they may be used in new rhythmic positions, and that they may even be turned upside down. This last happens to the motive with which the solo violin begins:

As the listener continues his exploration of polyphonic texture he will discover not only riches in musical styles which may have seemed foreign to his taste, but also an ability to hear his way through many passages in familiar music which formerly seemed barren. It frequently happens that the richest melodic lines are part of a complex strand of woven lines. Often the vitality of a melodic motive is so great that it seems to force the music to expand into a wider and more complex fabric. Certainly this is true of the jazz improvisation we mentioned earlier in the chapter; it is no less true of much other music.

Our new accomplishment, the ability to hear a polyphonic structure, leads directly to the next of the composer's resources, the next phase of musical language: harmony. The interwoven lines of a polyphonic texture result in vertical combinations of sounds which, whether they appear in music as the result of simultaneous melodic lines or as more nearly independent entities, deserve our attention.

RECORDINGS

John of Fornsete	"Sumer is icumen in"	Columbia 5715
Handy	"Yellow Dog Blues"	UHCH
Verdi	*Rigoletto:* "Bella figlia del- l'amore" (quartet)	Victor 10012
Bach	Concerto in D minor for two violins	Victor 7732, 7733

Chapter 6

HARMONY

THE word "harmony," musically speaking, is a word which usually appears as the title of a textbook describing, in highly technical fashion, the science of a certain kind of tonal relationships. That science is intensely interesting to the musician and forms part of the composer's equipment, but it is not one of the required prerequisites to listening. Part of the heritage of civilized life is the response which every normal person makes to harmonic combinations of sounds. Most people hear the harmony that belongs with familiar tunes even when it is not actually being produced. We notice it when an inexpert performer plays wrong chords in "America" or "The Star-Spangled Banner." Many of us can supply a barber-shop sort of harmony for songs which we know.

All this means that sounds in vertical combinations have some qualities to which we react. Our interest as listeners is simply to cultivate those reactions to the point where we will not miss any of the harmonic part of what the composer is saying. What can harmony do? Before this question can be answered completely we must consider something which applies not only to harmony but to melody and which is fundamental to them both: the relationships between tones.

The art of music could not exist without interrelationships of its sounds. The physicist can measure such relationships in terms of vibration, or they can be stated mathematically; more important, however, is the fact that they are perceptible to the normal ear. Indeed the ear takes in even more than the scientist can measure; it apprehends the pull of one tone toward or away from another. This tendency of sounds is what matters to the listener, and some understanding of it will carry him as near to a knowledge of harmony as he needs to come.

The sounds out of which is made the music of the Western world are such as fit into the relationship that we call *key*. Key, to the listener, needs to mean only one thing: a pattern which establishes a distinct level on which it functions. When music changes key, it changes level; but the important tonal relationships remain the same at the new level as they were at the old.

Most listeners have no difficulty in recognizing, not necessarily the name, but the tone that identifies the level of the music they are hearing. We have all had to be given the pitch for a song, or have had trouble finding the right pitch for a song we wanted to sing in the bathtub or at camp. We *feel* the center around which the other tones of a piece of music revolve. Sometimes we are not so adept in following a change to a new level when it is effected within a piece of music. Such a change of level or change of key is known to the musician as modulation; it is a process that is largely harmonic. Its importance to the listener is tremendous because it is so important to the fundamental architecture of music. It is mentioned now to indicate that the things we are examining have important implications for other aspects of music which we will discuss later.

A specific description of the relationships of tones within a key will be familiar to most listeners. To those for whom it is unfamiliar, it will not be difficult. The tone to which all others of the key relate themselves is the keynote or tonic —*do* to those who learned the scale by syllable. The position of the tonic determines the key level. For a soprano, the same song, for example, will have a higher tonic than for a bass. Centering on the tonic, the other tones fall into a scale-pattern group. Each tone has a function in that scale pattern which it gets from its relation to the tonic. This musical solar system behaves according to a kind of gravitational pull exerted by three tones, the tonic, the dominant, and the subdominant. The dominant is the *sol* of the syllable scale, five scale-tones above—or four below—the tonic. The sub-dominant is the *fa* of the scale, five scale-tones below—or four above—the tonic. These three tonal positions are the fundamental musical relationships. With the tonic as center they define the lines of gravitational pull of the whole circle of tones within the key:

TONIC, DOMINANT, SUBDOMINANT

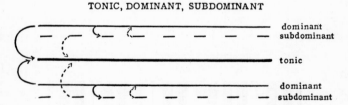

dominant
subdominant

tonic

dominant
subdominant

The importance of being able to hear the relationships to each other of tonic, dominant, and subdominant cannot be overemphasized. Western music is what it is because of them. They serve as the two piers and the keystone of the arch which supports our music.

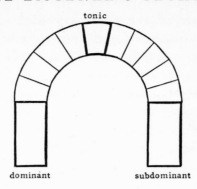

Learn them first as melodic positions. Sing or hum to yourself the following:

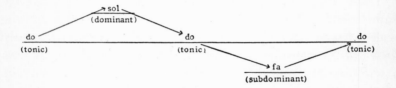

Feel the pull to return to the tonic from both dominant and subdominant. Play them on the piano:

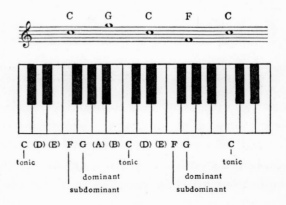

Using this picture of the piano keyboard if it is helpful, make up other sequences for the three tones. The relationships between them will become increasingly clear.

The pull which these three tones exert on each other owes its strength partly to listeners' having been conditioned to them not only as melodic elements or single points within a musical solar system but as the foundations for groups of tones sounding simultaneously as chords. Even when we sing them as single tones, our minds supply the missing sounds which fill out the chords.

These three chords within the musical solar system are fundamental. Together they contain all the sounds of the scale pattern which they represent. They represent the only *kinds* of harmony which are possible. Chords may take on a wide variety of qualities, but in *kind* they must partake of the pull of one of three: tonic, dominant, subdominant. They may be heard as the ending of every familiar hymn:

This discussion of positions in the scale and of the gravitational implications of those positions may, for the present, seem rather technical to anyone who wishes to listen for fun. But if it seems meager and incomplete to the listener who really wants to know about harmony, there is nothing to prevent his going to a textbook in harmony for more information. Harmony, to be of value to the listener, must be *heard*: it will have no value as a set of rules.

Here, then, we add to our former question asking what harmony can do—which we have not answered—a question that is bound up with it: How can we *hear* harmony? The answers to both questions will arrive together. We can get at them best by examining some pairs of words that describe both what harmony can do and how we hear what it does.

$$\begin{cases} \text{WIDE} \\ \text{NARROW} \end{cases}$$

Harmony can give the effect of a wide or a narrow ribbon of sound passing the point of consciousness. The sound of a violin or a flute playing a single melodic line would be narrow. Even here the narrowness would depend somewhat on the range of the melody. A massive chord in the orchestra with every instrument playing, from the low tuba and contra bassoon to the high piccolo, would be wide. The movement from narrow to wide, or from wide to narrow, is one of the composer's most powerful harmonic effects. Wagner's motive of "sleep magic," which can be heard in the music called "Wotan's Farewell and the Magic Fire" at the end of *The Valkyrie*,[1] conveys in terms of music that sensation of drawing together to a final single point of consciousness that many people experience when they fall asleep.

[1] Pp. 297, 298 in the vocal score published by G. Schirmer. Victor record 9176-B.

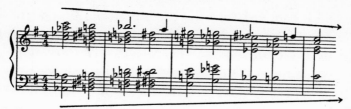

Here rhythm, melodic line, and tone-color are subordinated to the single effect: a harmonic procession from great width to extreme narrowness.

$$\begin{cases} \text{MAJOR} \\ \text{MINOR} \end{cases}$$

Here, again, are concepts which require somewhat technical explanation. Melodic lines may be in major or minor, and both melodic line and harmony may change from one to the other. The melodic and harmonic qualities described as major or minor grow out of the two kinds or *modes* of key that are common in Western music. Because a key mode is identified by its scale, the difference between major and minor can be illustrated with a ladderlike diagram:

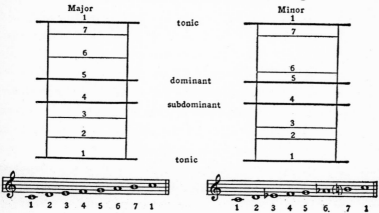

It should be noticed that the three positions of greatest importance—the tonic, dominant, and subdominant—remain the same for both modes. The pattern of whole steps and half steps is more complex in the minor mode than in the major, but harmonically the great difference appears in the shape of the chord on the tonic level. This chord consists, in either case, of the first, third, and fifth scale steps. Stated differently, it consists of the tonic, the dominant, and the tone halfway between the two. In major this middle tone is close to the one next above it:

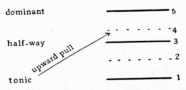

In minor it is close to the next one below it:

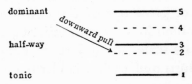

Among the tones in a key, as has already been suggested, the pull of the dominant and subdominant toward the tonic is so strong that it governs the whole tonal relationship. The attraction of any single tone toward the nearest scale tone is the next strongest pull. With this in mind, another glance at the diagrams of major and minor chords will show that the pull of the halfway tone in major is upward, while in minor it is downward.

In spite of the general notion of the matter, music in major is not always gay, nor is music in minor always sad— too many other factors are involved in producing a sense of gaiety or sadness. But the upward pull in major, the downward pull in minor, of the crucial tone in the tonic chord undoubtedly affects the feeling by which we distinguish major and minor.

Try the difference on the piano for yourself.

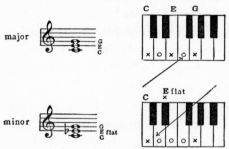

If you would enjoy making some musical experiments—how musical you can't tell until you try!—you might make up, or compose, some melodic motives on these two groups of tones. You might even attempt to use not only the keys marked with x but those marked with o. You will find, if your experience is normal, that the motives in major will have a characteristic upward motion, and that those in minor will be dominated by falling motion. This will demonstrate in another manner what has been described.

Certainly, one of the matters that are worth the listener's attention is the mode of a piece of music, the majorness or minorness of the harmony.

$$\left\{ \begin{array}{l} \text{ACTIVE} \\ \text{REST} \end{array} \right.$$

The gravitational pull which has been described in connection with single tones is really a kind of activity of those tones. Tones which are active tend to move toward points of rest. A like activity, with some added complexities, is characteristic also of harmonies. The harmony of the tonic is the center of gravity, the point of rest, toward which all other harmonies that can be associated with that key tend to move. Harmonic activity and rest are relative matters as much as the speed of forward movement; a chord active in one relationship may be a point of comparative rest in another. This apparent complexity is the source of much of the interest that harmony has for the listener. There is actually a kind of forward motion in harmony. This broad harmonic motion or rhythm will become apparent to many listeners only after some experience, but the perception is worth waiting for. It can be demonstrated with any phonograph record that is handy. Start it playing and then, with all of your attention on the fluctuation of the harmony between activity and rest, try to find a point of rest where you may lift the needle. Another exercise with which the listener may train his musical perception on this point involves the re-harmonizations of familiar tunes that can be heard on the radio and in the concert hall. The simplest and most normal harmonization of any melodic line follows the activity and rest implicit in that line. Such, for instance, are Stephen Foster's harmonizations of his melodies. The re-harmonizer sets up a new scheme of rest and activity and thus may be able to change the whole feeling of the melody itself. The arranger invariably does this with popular bands. It must be noted in passing, however, that the characteristic styles of popular bands are not due altogether to the harmonic qualities under discussion, but often are the result of an original instrumentation (tone-color) and highly individual rhythmic treatment.

$$\left\{ \begin{array}{l} \text{CONSONANT} \\ \text{DISSONANT} \end{array} \right.$$

Consonance and dissonance are very closely related to rest and activity, but the two pairs of words are not interchangeable. It is difficult, for instance, to imagine a dissonance that could convey a feeling of complete rest. Yet on the other hand, consonant harmonies may be active. There are long passages of music in which no dissonances are used, but the harmonic movement in them from activity to rest is perfectly clear. Of the qualities of harmony represented by this pair of words, consonance and dissonance, the latter is by far the most important to the listener. Dissonance may be regarded as a kind of harmonic activity that has the quality of tension. Physically, harmonies are consonant or dissonant as the vibrations which produce them reinforce each other or clash with each other. With a dissonance—and the greater the dissonance the truer is this statement—the ear has to struggle to hear the tones as belonging together. The dissonant sounds bump against each other in a kind of musical collision in which something must give way. The resulting tension can be released only by a movement of the tones away from each other; the ear fails to reconcile them. The bite of one tone on another, the resulting tension, and the final release of that tension by moving into another harmony constitute a drama enacted time after time, with varying degrees of poignancy, in almost any sort of music. It is one of the things that the listener must not miss. The second verse of the Bach Cantata No. 4, "Christ lay fast bound in Death's harsh chain" ("Christ lag in Todesbanden"), has the following magnificent passage:

There is nothing abrupt and unruly about these dissonances. The music is polyphonic, and the melodic lines move so smoothly that we have to listen for the clashes between them; if we miss the clashes, though, we haven't fully heard this music.

The reader may well ask at this point: "Am I actually being told to cultivate a sensitivity to the harsh, clashing, unmusical, modern aspect of music?" The answer is certainly yes! Tension is intolerable only when there is no possibility of release, and music would lose one of its greatest resources if it lost dissonance.

{ DIATONIC
{ CHROMATIC

The concepts represented by these words are not as strange to the listener as the words themselves may be. To make them clear we need only consider for a moment the structure of the scale. We have had a glimpse at the pattern into which sounds group themselves around the center established by key. That pattern is the diatonic scale; harmonies which use only the tones of the diatonic scale are diatonic harmonies. The normal harmony for a diatonic melodic line, such a one as that of "America," would be diatonic. The common harmonization of "America" is an excellent illustration of diatonic harmony, particularly because one very short chord departs from the diatonic—that on the second syllable of "liberty."

lib - er - ty

This departure from the normal diatonic harmony—almost every piece of music we know would show similar examples—is one of the most interesting of all harmonic resources. To understand it we must discuss chromatic harmony.

If one wishes to play a diatonic scale on the piano the easiest is the one that requires only white keys. Any other means dodging back and forth from white keys to black and skipping a white key when a black one is used. The reason is that a diatonic scale pattern uses both half steps and whole steps, and if the black keys were not there we could have a correct diatonic scale pattern only around one tonic center. All of which means this: In our music we actually use twelve sounds within each octave. Those twelve sounds, at half-step intervals, constitute the chromatic scale. Five of them are missing from the diatonic scale, but if the harmony is prevailingly diatonic some chromatic tones may be introduced without disturbing the sense of key level. The use of chromatic tones as part of the harmony makes the harmony chromatic. We hear commonly examples of every degree of chromaticism, from a piece like "America," with only one chromatic spot, to music so chromatic that our sense of tonal center feels as if it were riding on a roller coaster. For an example of music that is highly chromatic turn back to the Wagner sleep-magic motive on page 69.

This description of harmony will not give the listener a harmonic vocabulary unless he can hear the qualities that have been discussed. We hear harmony, however, in connection with tone-color, rhythm, and melodic line. A listening exercise in which harmony was the only element would hardly be music. Let us go on, then, to some music in which we can give most of our attention to harmonic qualities, but in which we must continue to apprehend others too.

RECORDINGS

Wagner   *The Valkyrie:* "Wotan's Farewell and the
         Magic Fire"   Victor 9176-B
Bach   Cantata No. 4: Verse II   Victor M-120

Chapter 7

HEARING MUSIC AS HARMONY

WE now have five points of reference for classifying what we hear harmonically. We have, in other words, a guide to the reactions we may expect harmony to produce in us. That guide consists of five pairs of words:

Wide	Major	Active	Consonant	Diatonic
Narrow	Minor	Rest	Dissonant	Chromatic

Surrounding all these is the basic quality of key level and the relationships that result from it. With this guide we can make the attempt to hear harmony, in the sense that hearing implies a conscious process of sorting out and reacting to what we hear.

Many composers have written music which is ideal for our present purpose. The kind of piece called theme and variations by composers seems created to give exactly the sort of practice that listeners need. In a theme and variations the composer takes a short and usually exceedingly simple but always complete piece of music as his theme. It may be a piece he has written himself, or it may be someone else's piece that he wishes he had written. After he gives us his theme he writes the piece over, as many times as he may wish, with changes each time. Each new and changed version of the theme is a variation. To have survived as part of musical literature, a theme and variations must be more than a stunt; it must be a whole in which the theme and its variations are contributory and meaningful parts.

HAYDN: "VARIATIONS ON THE 'EMPEROR' HYMN"

An excellent theme and variations for our purpose is one by Haydn on a theme that he had composed as a national hymn for his own country, Austria. The hymn has been borrowed by others for many purposes; Haydn's own borrowing of it for this piece lifts it above the temporary implications of some of its other associations. It is the second movement, the *Poco adagio cantabile* of the String Quartet in C major, Op. 76, No. 3. Because the hymn on which this movement is constructed begins with the words "God protect our Emperor" in conscious imitation of "God save the King," the whole quartet is commonly known as the "Emperor," and this particular movement is often called "Variations on the 'Emperor' Hymn."

Play the movement once to become familiar with its sound. If you do not already know the hymn, play the theme several times. Now—what can we learn from the variations? Let us take them one at a time.

THEME

On its first presentation, the theme shows a normal hymntune harmonization. Haydn makes no particular point of either wideness or narrowness in a texture that is distinctly monophonic. The theme is in major, and it remains in the same key. The alternation between rest and activity is normal. The only striking dissonance comes with the third note after the one that is held, and later when the same melodic group occurs again:

The harmonization is diatonic except for a mild chromaticism which is used three times: the subdominant is raised chromatically to make it point more strongly toward the dominant.

All in all, this theme is stated and harmonized in such a simple manner that a discussion of it can do little more than emphasize its simplicity. It should be mentioned that simplicity is the rule in a theme which is to be used for variations. A highly complex theme would be in danger of losing its identity during the process of variation.

VARIATION I

For this variation Haydn narrows his music to two lines. This does not narrow the complete fabric as much as the listener might expect, however, because of the wide range of the new part. The second violin plays the melody, the theme, and the first violin has to fill in the whole harmony. What the first violin does illustrates an interesting point about the way we hear harmony. In the statement of the theme the sounds which make up the chord are heard together:

melody

harmony

In the first variation they are heard one after the other, as they might be if they were played on a harp, and consequently they make up what is called an arpeggio (harp = *arpa* in Italian).

The listener hears that the harmony is stated differently, but also he hears that it is the same harmony. This single line of accompaniment, which is actually a new melodic line, is a device which makes possible the use of all the tones of the chords with which the main theme was originally harmonized. It adds, too, a new, rather simple polyphonic interest. As far as the actual chords are concerned, the first variation has the same harmony as the original statement of the theme. Into that harmony, however, as part of a new melodic line in the first violin, Haydn interjects a few chromatic and dissonant tones which add slightly to the harmonic activity.

In this first variation Haydn has already made his theme melody sound different. A good deal of the change is due to the rapid motion of the new part; that rapid motion is made possible by a new way of uttering the harmony, a way which allows for a slight increase of the harmonic activity.

VARIATION II

In this variation the melody is given a new tone-color by being played by the violoncello an octave lower than we heard it before. Otherwise it is exactly the same melody, except for a scale which Haydn interpolates just before the last high note, four measures from the end. Except, too, for a few low notes in the viola part, the melody is now at the bottom of the score. These changes have a tremendous effect in changing the sound of the music. In this variation, however, the composer goes even further. The first and second violin parts are really new melodic lines. The second violin moves with a rhythmic pattern quite similar to that of the melody, but the first violin is given much more freedom melodically, rhythmically, and harmonically. Here we meet not only the melodic and rhythmic, but the harmonic aspect of syncopation. The first violin holds a tone over from a harmony in which it fits to one with which it is dissonant. This continual holding back produces one dissonance, one point of extreme activity, after another.

In this variation we have, then, a new procession of harmonies, in a polyphonic texture which, because of the rhythmic independence of its lines, builds up a remarkably active harmonic fabric. Here is an excellent example of the way that the same melody may be given a quite different sound by a changed harmonic context.

VARIATION III

Here the melody is played by the viola, back in the same range where we first heard it. The accompaniment begins in the first violin with a new independent melodic line. The procession of harmonies is new. Until more than halfway through the variation only three instruments are playing. But we are hearing dissonances, resulting from syncopations, and chromaticisms which, even more than in the second variation, disguise the melody.

Listen to this variation carefully for the harmonic activity

that results from Haydn's use of chromaticism. The second
entrance of the violoncello is especially interesting:

Notice that although the melody is still major, the use of
chromaticism in the harmony has begun to destroy the distinction between the diatonic harmonies of major and minor.
The intensity and richness of this harmonization have resulted in changes in the qualities of activity, dissonance, and
chromaticism. It is a demonstration of considerable interest
to the listener.

VARIATION IV

In this final variation the theme melody returns to the
first violin and for all except its first four measures is heard
an octave higher than at any time before. Although the other
parts move to a higher range also, the effect is definitely
one of widening the harmony. In this music, where no matter how the harmony widens only four instruments are
playing, the effect is one of a kind of transparency.

The listener will be aware that Haydn has again changed
the whole harmonic progression. Dissonances and chromaticisms aid in this process. Haydn uses another device in this
variation that the listener will meet many times. Notice that
after the chromaticisms of the first seven and a half measures, the violoncello stays on the tonic, come what may in
the other parts, for four measures. This effect is called an

organ point, from the ease with which an organist can hold
one tone with a pedal while his hands are free to play other
harmonies. An organ point may be either a sustained or a
reiterated note. It has the double effect of producing dissonances against the harmonies with which it does not fit and
at the same time calling the listener's attention to the tonic.
Notice, finally, the extreme feeling of rest that Haydn
achieves for the final chord as a result of the long dissonant
passage which precedes it. The next to the last chord is an
excellent example of an extreme dissonance used for the sake
of the harmonic activity it can create. The listeners who
are aware of dissonance only through the so-called modern
music of our own time might take another look at this
chord:

Haydn died in 1809!

An understanding of how Haydn has used harmonic qualities in this set of variations should give the listener many
clues as to the interest he may expect to find in harmony.
Every piece of music that he hears will give more practice.

The musical process by which variations on a theme are
made is one from which the listener can obtain a great deal
of valuable enlightenment. It is a process in which the composer changes some of the elements of his original theme
while he retains others. He must not change too much, because he wants to keep his listener convinced that all the
music makes one whole. This aspect of a theme and variations implies an interesting question: How far can the com-

poser go in changing his musical material before the listener stops recognizing it? How much can the composer hide or disguise the tone-color, rhythm, melodic line, and harmony of his original theme and still expect the listener to follow what he is doing? From the standpoint of what we are trying to do the question must be asked in another way: How well can the listener follow the changes the composer is asking him to follow?

We are learning to hear harmony. But along with harmony go the other materials of which music is made. For our next exercise, another theme and variations, let us keep up the deliberate effort of learning to hear harmony. But let us, at the same time, follow changes that may take place as the variations develop.

SCHUBERT: VARIATIONS ON "DEATH AND THE MAIDEN"

The next music is a theme and variations by Schubert. It has several things in common with the Haydn piece. This, too, is for string quartet. Its theme is part of one of Schubert's own songs which he liked well enough to use again. The string quartet whose slow movement consists of this theme and variations is commonly known by the name of the song, "Death and the Maiden." Our interest, then, is in the theme and variations, based on a part of the song, "Death and the Maiden," from the String Quartet in D minor, Op. Posth.—a posthumous work, for this quartet, like a great deal of Schubert's music, was modestly packed away in a cupboard when a group of famous musicians found it rather difficult to read at sight, and it was not printed until after the death of its composer.

THEME

Here again the thematic material is presented with the utmost simplicity. The harmony is compact; the mode is minor. The balance between points of activity and rest is normal. There is very little dissonance. There are a few chromatic harmonies, especially near the end of the second half of the theme. What at first hearing appears as chromaticism is actually a shift in level; in the middle of the second half the music has actually moved to a new level, and the key is major. The diagram indicates what Schubert has done.

The effect of the final major chord should be noticed. It comes as a return to the first level, but defined now with a major harmony. This change from one level to another and then back again is a device of the utmost importance. The reaction to change in level, that is, to movement from one key to another, must be felt or else a musical value upon which the composer depends for much that he does will be missed. Listen to this theme several times for this one effect. Then follow it as it occurs in each variation.

The tone-color is that of strings. Within the string quartet, composers have been able to discover many subtle varieties of tone-color. Schubert here melts the strings together into a kind of compressed neutrality. Many variations on this basic quality will be possible.

Rhythmically and melodically, the music, of wholly monophonic texture, grows out of very simple motives. The first half of the theme has this, which returns near the end:

It is really only one motive:

The second part adds another pair of notes to this motive, and now a new, longer motive has actually grown out of the original one:

As we make the acquaintance of the variations we will have to follow the manner in which Schubert changes these motives.

VARIATION I

After the somber theme this first variation must impress the listener by its complete change of atmosphere. It sounds almost like a new piece of music. How much of the theme is left in it, and how much is new? It is still minor, and the careful listener will discover that the procession of harmonies is exactly the same as for the theme. If he listens carefully he will discover, too, that the rhythm of the motives has been retained at the bottom of the music. The violoncello part is exactly as it was for the theme except that here it is plucked—played *pizzicato*—while originally it was played with the bow:

This bottom line of the music, by continuing the outline of both the original motives and the harmony, is what ties this variation to the theme. All the other parts, except as what they play belongs to the harmony, have something new.

The second violin and viola introduce a completely new scheme of forward motion. Each beat is now divided into a group of three; this triplet motion gives the variation the feeling of being much faster music:

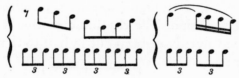

The first violin is given a new melodic line, a kind of obbligato that adds width to the fabric and at the same time attracts our attention by its lacy decorativeness. The rhythmic conflict between this line and the triplets of the interior parts adds to the restlessness of the forward motion. At several points the motion is two against three or four against three:

It should be noticed that the fabric of the music has become polyphonic. More important, the listener is asked to connect much new material with a remnant of the theme that is partly hidden in the bottom of the music. If he does not make that connection, he has difficulty in understanding this as a variation of the theme. When it is understood as a variation the listener must feel that Schubert has started a musical process in which he is attempting to dissect away from his original idea many of its somber, slow-moving, and almost colorless implications. It is as though he said to us, of this first variation: "Now, just wait a moment; the meaning of my theme is not all on the surface. It has the power to attract to itself strength and vitality and new kinds of beauty. We must hear what it implies before we understand it."

Here we get a glimpse into the real magic of music.

VARIATION II

The second variation is a further elaboration of the same procession of harmonies used so simply in the theme. The bottom of the fabric is now filled in by the viola. If the listener follows it closely he will hear that the bass has not changed harmonically. It has changed rhythmically, however, and here Schubert uses an interesting device. The first variation introduced a heightened rhythmic vitality without changing the basic motive which continued in the bass. That rhythmic strength, as though infectious, penetrates the bass in the present variation. The rhythmic motive is now twice as fast; its time values have been cut in half so that it is heard twice as often:

In this variation, too, the motive has so much energy that it jumps an octave, to look like this:

Against the new version of the motive, the first and second violins continue the development of rhythmic excitement with lines that have slight melodic significance but contain new rhythmic patterns:

These two lines, with the bass in the viola, outline the harmony.

The violoncello, playing rather high in its range, has the outstanding melodic line of this variation. It begins like this:

The listener will immediately hear that this new melodic line uses the main motive of the theme, but uses it to sing a different song.

One other point is worth the listener's notice. Two forms of the original theme motive are being heard at the same time during this variation—one in the violoncello's melodic line and one in the bass which the viola plays:

The magic gathers momentum.

VARIATION III

In this variation the rhythmic vitality which Schubert finds in the original motive reaches a climax. It now is four times as fast as at first:

The listener has been asked to follow a process of rhythmic multiplication.

It is a device that we will meet time after time, and it should not be hard for us to follow this kind of musical derivation. We have no difficulty in recognizing the constants in non-musical processes of acceleration involved in operating machines of various kinds.

At first all four instruments play this new version of the theme motive. After four measures the music suddenly becomes quieter, and the highest and the lowest parts make short melodic excursions which are reminiscent of the melodic line of the second variation. In the middle of the variation the music again rises in intensity, and the two outside parts alternate with heavy chords:

The variation ends abruptly with the same motive, in all the parts, with which it began.

The listener will be aware that he has witnessed a remarkable musical transmutation in the rhythmic progression from the original theme through these first three variations. The basic harmony has remained the same, but the temper of the music has changed completely.

VARIATION IV

Now we have a partial return to the initial mood of the theme, but elements of earlier excitement remain, and the harmony has changed to major. Schubert no longer adheres so strictly to the original procession of harmonies. It is as though the harmony, which has stayed constant through a tremendous process of development, now relaxes its hold on the musical fabric a little.

The motive appears in its first rhythmic shape:

The first violin weaves a delicate tracery around the rest of the smooth, light fabric.

VARIATION V

The final variation returns to minor. To compensate for the harmonic excursions of the previous variation and—if we know the habits of composers—to foretell the approach of the end of the piece, this variation begins with an organ point on the tonic level. Rhythmically, the organ point transfers the pattern of the first violin part of Variation IV to the bottom of the music as if to give it another function before it disappears:

Above this organ point the viola and second violin have lines that are reminiscent of former uses of the theme motive. The first violin soon begins a pattern of four rapid notes, against three in the violoncello:

The first violin becomes louder and soon is so insistent that the second violin and viola second its rhythm. At this point the violoncello has an interesting melodic variation of the second original motive:

This, it might be noticed in passing, is exactly the sort of improvisational melodic variation that is heard so often in the "jam" choruses of popular music. It has an infectious quality here. Before it ends the second violin part transfers some of the excess energy into an interesting syncopation:

Schubert was not a swing musician, but he knew that nothing else would serve to fill this climax with exuberance as a tipping over of the rhythm would.

At this point begins the process which will bring us smoothly to the end. Notice that as the music softens the motion begins to disappear.

And the motion finally disappears with this faltering passage:

While the slowing down proceeds, the original theme motive returns. As it pushes everything else aside we hear it finally in all the parts, at first high and then at the end back in the range where it was heard at the very beginning. The music at last arrives at a point of rest in major after a chord that has a dissonant activity much like what Haydn used in ending his final variation.

This rather short passage at the end has a completely different feeling from the original presentation of the theme, of which it is obviously reminiscent. That is part of the plan of the piece. If the listener has followed what Schubert is making the music do from one variation to the next he will realize that all the intervening music would be wasted, its argument lost, if the end sounded like the beginning.

In this chapter the listener has made the acquaintance of two memorable pieces of music. More than that, he has made considerable advance toward greater ease and exactness of hearing. He is learning the language.

Tone-color, rhythm, melodic line, harmony—these are the parts of musical speech. But we must now turn our attention to matters beyond the bare bones of grammar.

RECORDINGS

Haydn	String Quartet in C major, Op. 76, No. 3: Poco adagio cantabile	Columbia Set 246
Schubert	String Quartet in D minor, Op. Posth. ("Death and the Maiden"): Andante con moto	Victor M-468

Chapter 8

STYLE

MOST listeners are more aware of musical style than they realize. Certainly the distinct styles of many of our popular dance bands are familiar, as a matter of everyday recognition, to many people who also go to concerts. Arrangers for dance bands make over the pieces their band plays to fit a preconceived style. The musical elements are exactly the same for them as for any composer. The style that we connect with a composer or a popular band is the result of the way that the composer or arranger uses tone-color, rhythm, melodic line, and harmony in each particular selection.

For the listener, a consideration of style is simply another way of looking at what we have been studying. It is a viewpoint that ties all the elements of music together, where they belong. When we hear music, one of the definite impressions we get is that of style. Our aim here is to increase our ability to receive a *true* impression of style. Musical style is, then, the sum total, for any given piece or composer or period, of the kind of musical materials that have been used.

There are two major determinants of musical style. The first of these is the kind of musical materials available at the time the music was composed. The second is the taste and ability of the composer. Each factor deserves some attention. An understanding of their influence will enrich the listener's concept of style, and an explanation of their functioning will help to explain stylistic differences.

An analogy from another art will help to clarify the statement that musical style is determined in part by the kind of materials available at the time of composition.

During the period when Europe was building its Gothic cathedrals one of the objects of the architects was great height. The only materials available were stone and brick, tied together with plaster and lead or held in place by gravity. The builders wrought magnificently with them and raised the highest structures the world was to know for centuries. We can now build higher, however, because we have discovered how to make and use steel girders and reinforced concrete. New materials have come into use. The Empire State Building could not have been erected eight hundred years ago, because the necessary materials were not known.

The same rule can be demonstrated time after time in music. Such a demonstration grows out of our understanding of the history of music, which is, essentially, the story of the gradual accumulation of musical materials. In minute detail, this story is not a necessary prerequisite to, nor can it be a substitute for, hearing music. From what it has to tell, however, we can learn in general what materials were available to composers at any given time.

Let us examine a few samples.

For centuries the chief function of music was liturgical. Music makers had so few materials available that music independent of a verbal text was beyond their imagination. The human voice was the only important musical instrument. The rhythm of music was the rhythm of the words of a text. Harmony as we know it was nonexistent. Our scales too were unknown, and such scales as were in use were governed by principles which we would consider arbitrary. Music consisted solely of a melodic line. Even the mechanics of writing music were primitive. What music has survived in primitive notation is in one definite style, the *plain song*. Much of it remains in use in the liturgy of the Roman Catholic Church. Here is an example: [1]

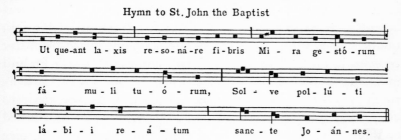

Hymn to St. John the Baptist

At another stage, much later, harmonic and rhythmic materials had become available. Musicians had begun their discovery of harmony by weaving melodic lines together; they had, in other words, learned how to manage a polyphonic fabric. To give independence to the lines of the fabric they found it necessary to adapt to music a kind of rhythm which they found in poetry. The resultant independence of the melodic lines gave them a kind of harmony. To make the harmony pleasant these early musicians were compelled to make changes which led finally to our modern system of key relationship with its scales and chords. Tone-color was still largely restricted to the human voice, but they were making remarkable discoveries in flexibility of the tone-color that could be produced by choral singing. All this describes, on the basis of the availability of materials, a musical style

[1] This Hymn may be heard on Victor record 20897. Note that when the singers begin to hold the first syllable of each phrase the result is no longer characteristic of the plain-song style.

entirely different from plain song. Any of the motets, madrigals, or masses of Palestrina, Lasso, Vittoria, Byrd—in fact, any of the choral music of the sixteenth century—will illustrate this style.

Another stopping place far removed could be illustrated by means of a Prelude and Fugue for pipe organ by J. S. Bach (1685-1750).[2] When we come to Bach's period, however, it becomes increasingly clear that the immense accumulation of musical materials at hand at any given time could not possibly be displayed in any one piece of music or even in all the music of any one composer. But a Prelude and Fugue for organ by Bach will be useful in showing some of the many materials, not in use in the sixteenth century, that were available to Bach.

In the first place the Prelude and Fugue is music written for an instrument that has considerable flexibility and range of tone-color—think of the mechanical inventions that were required for that! It is not written to a text, which means that musical materials had to win their independence; they must now get along by themselves. They do it in a number of ways. The melodic lines move in a measured, accented rhythm and grow out of definite motives; the polyphonic fabric is controlled harmonically, with a kind of harmony that is definitely based on the relations of chords within a key. Harmony, moreover, has arrived at the point where free movement from one key to another is possible.

The music of Bach, considered only as it represents a stage in the accumulation of musical materials, exhibits those materials—tone-color, rhythm, melodic line, harmony—as forming a style impossible to the time of Palestrina. The effect of accumulation can be seen with even more clarity

---

[2] Prelude and Fugue in E minor, recorded by Albert Schweitzer (Victor 9741).

in the matter of instrumental performance. The ability a composer demands of his performers certainly determines in part what he writes. Increased flexibility of performance has depended on two factors: first, improvements in instruments; second, advancement in playing technic. The composer's materials were enriched when valves were added to the trumpet and French horn, when more keys and levers were devised for the woodwinds, and when the range of the piano was increased. No generation of performers has been satisfied if it did not surpass its teachers in the technic of performance.

Accumulation has continued, and the process has been accompanied by tremendous changes in musical style. The tone-color resources of the modern symphony orchestra have been discovered since the time of Bach. The orchestras of Mozart (1756-1791), of Beethoven (1770-1827), and of Wagner (1813-1883) each represent a distinct tone-color style, and the listener will find from experience that the list can be made much longer. Harmonic style, in like manner, has undergone a long series of changes. How toleration of dissonance has increased will be obvious from a comparison of, for instance, the first movement of Beethoven's Seventh Symphony with the final scene, "The Sacrificial Dance," of Stravinsky's "Rite of Spring" ("Sacre du Printemps"). The two works were composed almost exactly one hundred years apart. Part of the process which has brought about what some listeners, when they hear music like Stravinsky's, will feel to be a complete disappearance of the harmonic horizon, has been the increase in the use of chromaticism. This can be heard by comparing the Beethoven movement mentioned above with, for example, the first movement of the Franck Symphony in D minor (1889).

These comparisons should be made. It is not enough to read about them or hear them mentioned. Play these pieces and listen for their different-*sounding* styles—styles that differ in sound because of the absence or presence of certain kinds of musical material:

1. Plain song	Hymn to St. John the Baptist	Victor 20897
2. Palestrina	*Missa Papae Marcelli:* Sanctus and Hosanna	Columbia 5712
3. Bach	Prelude and Fugue in E minor	Victor 9741
4. Mozart	Symphony No. 39 in E flat major: first movement	Victor M-258
Beethoven	Fourth Symphony: first movement	Columbia M-197 Victor M-274
Wagner	*Die Meistersinger:* Prelude to Act I	Columbia 68854-D
5. Beethoven	Seventh Symphony: first movement	Victor M-317
Stravinsky	"Rite of Spring" ("Sacre du Printemps"): "Sacrificial Dance"	Victor M-74
6. Beethoven	Seventh Symphony: first movement	Victor M-317
Franck	Symphony in D minor: first movement	Victor M-300

A composer's taste and ability also determine the style of his music. Within the restrictions laid upon him by the state of musical materials at the time in which he lives, the free play of the composer's personality is supreme. He may reject some of the materials that his contemporaries are using, as many of our present composers reject the advanced harmonic idiom of Schoenberg. He may, on the other hand, venture beyond the accepted materials of his own time, as almost every great composer has done—lesser composers have done it too, but their music is forgotten. He may find, as a result of his training and interest, or because of the opportunities for performance presented to him, that certain current fashions in music do not interest him. A composer who spends his life working with choirs, for instance, might never write for the symphony orchestra. Another composer might

devote himself entirely to mastering the intricacies of writing for the orchestra.

Most composers develop mannerisms in their use of musical materials. These may consist of a favorite chord or a
favorite rhythmic or melodic device. How many times does
one recognize the music of Handel because the harmonic
progressions are reminiscent of the Largo? As the listener
makes the acquaintance of more and more of the music of
any one man he will become aware of that composer's mannerisms for himself. As he does discover them, he will have
reason for self-congratulation, because it will indicate a
growing ability to perceive musical style. As a kind of hobby
the search for the elements of a composer's personal idiom
can be fascinating. Virgil Thomson, in his book *The State
of Music,* develops an interesting theory to the effect that a
composer's style is influenced by the source of his income.
Such a theory, whether it is right or wrong, could originate
only with a person who is extremely sensitive to musical
style.

As a concept that brings together all the different sorts
of things that tones can do, musical style has another important implication for the listener. There may be some
question as to whether the source of a composer's income
directly affects his style, but there can be little doubt of
the influence of his personality on it.

For those to whom music has become a familiar language,
it is axiomatic that great music can be composed only by
men who are essentially great. Granting that a composer
has the ability to accomplish what he wants to do, it is his
purpose that will give the measure of his greatness. Does he
crave little moments or great moments for his listeners? Does
he wish to be heard in the night club, the supper room, or

at the symphony concert? Does he associate his music with the aspects of life that are eternal and sublime or with those that are base and degenerate? Does he write one opera inspired by fidelity and devote his final symphony to the concept of human brotherhood? [3] Or is he satisfied to be included in the Hit Parade? Music has many functions, and for each a purpose. Each function and each purpose has its own dignity: Beethoven did not demean himself when he composed popular dance music, but his greatness is much more apparent in the symphony which has been called an apotheosis of the dance.[4]

The composer's purpose, then, will be a qualifying factor in the style of his music. Ability to perceive style completely in listening, and with it its intimations of purpose, comes only with experience. Neither this chapter nor any chapter that has ever been written can teach it. At best, this chapter can prepare the listener for it. Style is implicit in what a composer makes his tones do, and hearing style is hearing what tones do.

Every piece of music the listener hears may be an exercise in musical style. At the present point, however, some listening should be deliberately devoted to objectifying the hearing of style. Style is a result of what tones do, the tones considered as tone-color, rhythm, melodic line, and harmony. The result, a kind of sum of all that happens in the music or a kind of individual imprint superimposed on the whole, may give intimations not only of the time when the music was written, but of the quality and purpose—and identity —of the composer.

[3] Beethoven, *Fidelio;* Ninth Symphony.
[4] Beethoven, Seventh Symphony.

An illuminating exercise consists of making a comparison
of the styles of two pieces of music—any two pieces by composers who lived at different times. Try these:

Handel   Recitative, "For, behold, darkness shall
              cover the earth" and air, "The people
              that walked in darkness," from *The
              Messiah*   Columbia 68604-D,
                                                                    68605-D
Wagner   "Prize Song," from *Die Meistersinger*   Victor 7105

Play each several times. Try to answer questions like the following as you listen:

How do the two pieces compare as to tone-color?
    What makes the orchestras sound different?
    Which orchestra has more instruments?
    Which orchestra has the larger variety of instruments?
    Which piece makes the greater demands on the players?
    What class of voice is singing?

How do the two pieces compare rhythmically?
    To what degree, in each piece, is the emphasis on the basic
        measure?
    Is the basic measure obscured at any time in either piece?
    Are there changes from one rhythm to another?
    How much syncopation is there?
    Do you hear, in either piece, rhythms that conflict with
        the basic measure?
    What is the measure?

How do the melodic lines of the two pieces compare?
    Do you hear places in either piece where the verbal text
        is so important that the composer does not use melodic
        motives?
    What are the important melodic motives in each piece?

How are they used?

Do you hear simultaneous melodic lines in either piece?

Is the fabric monophonic or polyphonic?

Does it change from one to the other?

Do the melodic lines have a characteristically rising or falling inflection?

How does the harmony of the two pieces compare?

Wide?

Narrow?

Major?

Minor?

Active?

Rest?

Consonant?

Dissonant?

Diatonic?

Chromatic?

Do not try to answer questions regarding the personal qualities of the styles represented by these two pieces. You do not have data enough with one piece from a composer. Remember these two songs as being Handel's and Wagner's. The recollection of them will start your feeling for the styles of these two composers. As far as you dare to go is to ask yourself if the purpose of each of these pieces, as indicated by the verbal text, has been served with understanding, dignity, and ability.

RECORDINGS

Hymn to St. John the Baptist		Victor 20897
Palestrina	*Missa Papae Marcelli:* Sanctus and Hosanna	Columbia 5712
Bach	Prelude and Fugue in E minor	Victor 9741

Mozart	Symphony No. 39 in E flat major	Victor M-258
Beethoven	Fourth Symphony	Columbia M-197
		Victor M-274
Wagner	*Die Meistersinger:* Prelude to Act I	Columbia 68854-D
Beethoven	Seventh Symphony	Victor M-317
Stravinsky	"Rite of Spring" ("Sacre du Printemps"): "Sacrificial Dance"	Victor M-74
Franck	Symphony in D minor	Victor M-300
Handel	*The Messiah:* "For, behold, darkness shall cover the earth"; "The people that walked in darkness"	Columbia 68604-D
		Columbia 68605-D
Wagner	*Die Meistersinger:* "Prize Song"	Victor 7105

Chapter 9

FORM

NEARLY everyone knows what it feels like to get lost. The first visit to a new city is marked by the feeling of being a stranger. An attempt to find the way from railroad station to hotel or to go sightseeing usually ends in an appeal for help. The visitor from the Middle West doesn't understand why he can't walk around the block in Boston, or the resident of Syracuse can't understand the numbering of the buildings in New York City. The stranger is always lost. Unless he is stubborn, or has more time than he knows how to use, or just isn't interested, he will buy a guidebook or a map. He will learn the plan of the strange place, and when he does he won't get lost.

Everyone who has listened to music knows how it feels to be lost. Hardly any listener can hear music that is new to him—not music of any great length, certainly—without getting lost. He takes in some of the most striking motives near the beginning, perhaps, but as the music proceeds his impressions become increasingly vague, and finally his attention drifts from the music and he is lost. He feels as if he were swimming in a sea of sound, with no shore in sight. No wonder some music seems long! The pleasure is spoiled when the listener has lost his bearings.

The stranger in a new city might eventually learn his way

about—by himself, with no outside help—if he got lost in
enough places and remembered each time how he finally set
himself right. The listener hearing a new piece of music
might do the same: repeated hearings would finally bring
the insight of familiarity. A map would hasten the process
in the first case. Is there anything that may be used as a map
by the listener?

Musical form has many aspects. It has been described and
studied from several different standpoints. For the listener it
has some important implications which need not enter the
present discussion. Its great value here is that it can help
keep us from getting lost. An understanding of musical form
can prepare the listener to recognize *what is coming next* in
a piece of music. It has the same relation to music as a map
has to a city.

For many experienced listeners musical form is a much
stronger support than a map can ever be. If we can discover
at the outset a way to use form as a guide to complete musical experience, we can soon forget it as a concept in any
degree separate from music and discover that it is, in fact,
the very shape of the musical experience.

As we begin, we need to add a word to the vocabulary
of our musical discussion, the word "phrase." For our present purpose, a phrase is the amount of music that can be
sung in one breath. The breath may be long or short. The
music may even be performed entirely by instruments not
affected by our breathing. Constituted as we are, it is natural
for us to use an expression that relates to our breathing in
referring to the fragments of sense into which our ideas may
be broken. Omit the breath, or the pause that allows for it,
in stating an idea; and the peculiar sense of tension or ex-
haustion such an omission will produce will show how in-

stinctively we use the length of our breath as a norm in speech, in thought.

Let us examine the phrases of a simple piece of music. Delightful for this purpose is an old French love song, "Mon cœur se recommande à vous" ("My heart commends itself to thee") composed by Orlando Lasso in 1560. It can be heard, sung with lute accompaniment, on a Victor record. Play it.

The first phrase, a kind of introduction by the lute, has the following melodic line:

In order to remember the identity of the phrases as they follow each other, let us assign letters to them as they come. The first phrase will be *a;* each succeeding phrase, if it is different from any we have heard, will be given a new letter; if it is a repetition of a former one, it will be given the same letter as at its first appearance.

As we follow through the song, listening for the places where the singer breathes, we will arrive at a letter pattern about as follows:

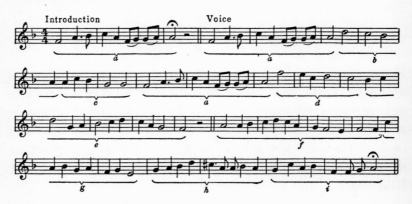

If this is not clear at first, play the song several times. There might be some difference of opinion as to where to put the letters—some phrases are short, and some, like *e*, are quite long. Now let us make a row of these letters which represent phrases:

a|abcadefghiabcade

Our notice is first attracted to the recurrences of *a*. Not counting the introduction, it appears four times. Twice it occurs in the grouping *abc* and twice in that of *ade*. We see that *abc* and *ade* together form a section which appears twice, once at the beginning and once at the end, with the section *fghi* between. Thus we have a pattern like this:

a abcade　fghi　abcade

The pattern for sections is as follows:

A　　　B　　A
a|abcade　fghi　abcade

Notice that section *A* is closely knit, with two appearances of phrase *a,* while section *B*, in the middle, introduces one new phrase after another. Such freedom in the middle section is not necessary, but is possible because of the close knitting of the outside sections. It has, moreover, the effect of making the return of section *A* feel more like a kind of homecoming.

Here, in this simple three-section or ternary form, we get a glimpse of an important formal principle: *repetition after contrast*. Repetition after contrast, which can be represented by the formula *ABA,* is basic to most of the music we hear. It is hardly fair, however, to insist on deducing a general principle from only one example. Let us add to our experience.

Another interesting little love song, this time in Italian, is one composed by Alessandro Scarlatti, "O cessate di pia-garmi" ("O no longer seek to pain me"). This too can be heard on a Victor record. Several hearings will give this analysis:

$$A \quad\quad B \quad\quad A$$
$$abb \quad cccdd \quad abb$$

There may be some disagreement as to the small letters representing phrases. Recall that we are mapping the melodic line, and then remember how a new harmonization may change the effect of a melody. If we took phrase variation into account, we would have this result:

$$abb^1 \quad cc^1c^2dd^1 \quad ab^2b^3$$

The phrase variations, which add so much interest, do not, however, change the general picture beyond recognition.

Notice that this song begins and ends in minor, that both *A* sections are in the same minor key. But the feeling of a harmonic return from a distant point to the level of the beginning is very marked at the last chord of section *B*. Where has the music wandered, harmonically? We need not answer that question technically. It is sufficient to be aware that the harmony, too, is at last making a repetition after contrast.

'A return to the initial level of the harmony, the key of the
beginning, after a modulation or excursion away from it,
is one of the most powerful supports of musical form. We
first met it in our study of variations. Learn to watch for it.

Let us turn next to a piece of instrumental music in an
entirely different style. The music of this chapter is excellent
for the kind of style comparisons that were suggested in the
previous chapter. We can now do our listening from another
viewpoint. Let us give our attention to the main outlines of
the form, to the sections for which we have used capital letters in our diagrams. As we recognize the sections we will
characterize them as to tone-color, rhythm, melodic motives,
and harmony. Try to catalogue mentally the most notable
characteristics of the music. Usually they will cluster around
the striking melodic motives, which are the substance out
of which the phrases grow.

Play a record of the "Dance of the Flutes" from Tchaikovsky's "Nutcracker" Suite. Its general form is the now
familiar *ABA* structure. *A*, in major, is enunciated by three
flutes. The most important melodic motive is heard at the
beginning:

This motive is used in a variety of phrases, but, with the help
of the flute tone-color, there is no difficulty in recognizing
it. *B* is in minor, on a level distinctly different from *A*. The
low instruments insist on the new level with a kind of organ
point, a constant, almost monotonous reiteration of *do, sol
do, sol do:*

do sol do sol do

The brass instruments furnish the tone-color that marks this section, although before it is finished most of the instruments of the orchestra, except the flutes, are playing. The melodic motive, as in section *A*, is made of rapid notes:

The return of section *A* brings back the flutes, with their characteristic motive, and the original major key level.

The listener will soon discover and remember, further, that the second section *A* is shorter than the first, and that some interesting things that were heard the first time are missing from the repetition after *B*.

It soon becomes apparent that the first *A* had subsections, longer than phrases, but characteristic units in themselves. The first of these units presents the flute trio over a subordinate accompaniment. The second subsection shunts the flute trio, still playing its characteristic motive, into the background, and gives the front of the stage to the English horn, with a short but completely new melodic line:

This momentary contrast, which ends with four descending notes in the bass clarinet, gives way to the original flute music, which returns, in a short passage, to the foreground. But when the flutes again sing their original music, the whole fabric is made heavier by the strings, which imitate the flutes:

Actually, then, the pattern for this piece is a slight variation of the very simple ternary form, with a kind of sub-
ternary plan used for the first section. In this diagram the
small letters represent subsections, not phrases.

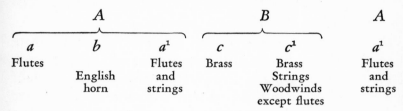

	A			*B*		*A*
a	*b*	*a*¹	*c*	*c*¹		*a*¹
Flutes		Flutes	Brass	Brass		Flutes
	English	and		Strings		and
	horn	strings		Woodwinds		strings
				except flutes		

The interested listener will discover that in this piece, as
in most music, the ternary principle—repetition after contrast—can be followed into even smaller divisions of music
than have been discussed. What is more important, he will
have noticed that repetition after contrast can (and often
does) apply to all of the composer's materials. Tchaikovsky
contrasts tone-color, melodic line, rhythmic style, harmonic
level, mode, and style. By the simple device of keeping the
rapid motion going, and by returning to music like the beginning, he convinces the listener that it all belongs together.

This chapter should close with a suggestion that the listener now test what his knowledge of form has done for him.
Play again the three pieces we have studied. Is it not true
that what you have observed of their structure gives you a
completely different feeling about the music? You are ap-
proaching a concept of music as existing in a different kind
of space from that which was discussed earlier in the book
and which may be called simply time. Music exists in the
mind-space of the listener. What is heard at the moment of
consciousness can be *related* to what has gone before and to
what is coming.

Do not expect this one small pattern to apply to all the music you hear. Do not expect to be able to pick it out immediately in any music you hear; it will make itself plain to you only in music in which it has been consciously used by the composer. We learn a new language slowly. *Es war einmal ein Mann*—"Once there was a man"—is the first sentence in an old reader for beginning students of German. It is a statement that does not fit into very many real situations. But it is a beginning, and eventually the principle of sentence structure in *Es war einmal ein Mann* will be found to have a universal application.

The ternary (*ABA*) principle in music has an almost universal application because composers have learned how to expand it into large and complex musical forms. We now turn to an examination of those larger forms.

RECORDINGS

Lasso	"Mon cœur se recommande à vous"	Victor 20228
Scarlatti	"O cessate di piagarmi"	Victor 21747
Tchaikovsky	"Nutcracker" Suite: "Dance of the Flutes"	Victor M-256

Chapter 10

THE RONDO

THERE is no limit to the variety of ways in which the simple ternary principle may be made to serve in extended pieces of music. But several varieties of extension have become so traditional that the listener will meet them time after time. The rondo is the least complex of these.

The rondo is probably a "folk" invention. Imagine a group of people singing, clapping their hands, and dancing a short refrainlike song. Between each two refrains a solo singer or a solo dancer improvises music for his own contribution. After each solo the group does the refrain. Such a piece could last all night. Many folksongs must owe their almost endless length and variety to some such process. If we apply the same scheme of using letters as before, we get a diagram like this:

A	*B*	*A*	*C*	*A*	
					etc.
refrain	solo	refrain	solo	refrain	

This is the basic design for a rondo. The process of repetition after contrast keeps on going. Though fundamentally it is extremely simple, the rondo may develop considerable complexity, and it will take several examples to exhibit its possibilities fairly.

Before we go on, however, we may as well learn a new and very useful expression: thematic material. We have discussed the materials of music and listened for them sufficiently to be able to hear them. We know that a composer's interest may shift from one aspect of his material to another. Whatever material he may concentrate on for a desired effect, this we may call his thematic material. It will contain his melodic motives, and it will have some special rhythmic, harmonic, or color significance. It may be similar to the theme in a theme and variations. The expression "thematic material" will be used to include whatever musical material, be it motive, rhythmic pattern, harmonic progression, or special tone-color, the composer has chosen as subject matter.

For our first rondo, let us examine the Entr'acte from Schubert's *Rosamunde*. Play a record of it.

Section *A* is based on thematic material which Schubert liked well enough to use in three different pieces. He uses it for a string quartet movement (String Quartet in A minor, Op. 29) and, in a slightly different form, as a theme for variations in the Impromptu in B flat for piano.

This is the important motive:

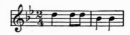

You will notice that section *A* has two subsections with a different use of the thematic material in each. In the first subsection the original motive is answered by another.

In the second subsection the motive, with a different melodic shape, is used by itself:

Notice, too, that a new key level is established just before
the second subsection and that the harmonic journey back
to the original level at the end of the section furnishes some
interesting progressions. Section *A* could be plotted like this:

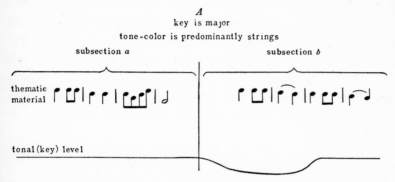

For section *B* the music changes abruptly to minor on another key level; in this case, the relative minor.[1] Along with
the change to the relative minor come changes in tone-color
and rhythm. The thematic material is this:

With this accompanying rhythm:

The melodic line moves interestingly from one woodwind
instrument to another. Like section *A*, this one has two dis-

[1] See Appendix, pages 335, 338.

tinct subsections. The triplet motion of the motive is followed, in the second subsection, by a measure in duple motion (the beat divided into two instead of three parts):

The harmonic plan of section *B* is interesting. At the end of the first subsection the listener is made to think that there has been a modulation. But it is a deception and the music returns immediately to the level which characterizes the section.

Section *B* could be plotted as follows:

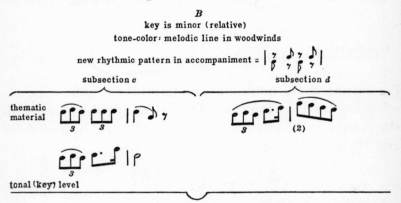

Section *A* returns, after *B*, exactly as it was heard at first. Then follows section *C*.

Section *C* is in minor, and the listener will feel that this is a more distinct minor than what he heard in section *B*. The reason for this impression is that although the music has changed to minor it has not changed key level. The contrast between major and minor is greater when it is made without changing key level.

With the change to minor this section again emphasizes

the tone-color of the woodwinds. The thematic material is new, although its triplet is reminiscent of section *B*:

This motive continues through both subsections. The accompaniment is based on a new rhythm:

Here is the diagram of section *C*:

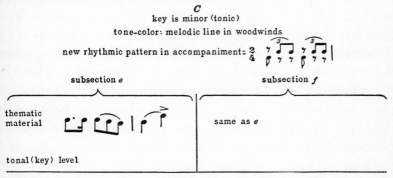

After section *C* the music returns to section *A*, with which the piece ends. This rondo divides into five parts, and the whole piece has the following form:

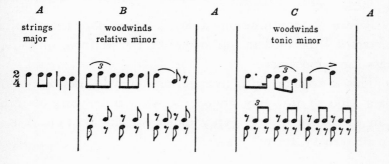

The listener should notice, before we turn to another rondo, that section *A* of the Schubert piece comes to a complete stop each time it ends. It never leads to the next section, and the change from *A* to *B* or from *A* to *C* is always rather sudden and abrupt. The result of this is that when *A* stops for the third time, which is the end of the piece, it uses an ending that has been heard twice before. This is not the usual procedure. As a general rule the sections of a rondo are connected smoothly; the endings for section *A* lead up to what follows, and so when the end of the piece is reached, a period must be put to this suggestion of something more to come. The composer must fashion an ending, a *coda*. The coda has the function of a brake on the forward motion of the music. It can be either long or short, depending on what the momentum demands. It must be composed so cleverly that the listener will not have the feeling of hurtling through the windshield that results from applying the brakes too suddenly. In our next rondos we must observe the bridges between the sections, the relation of the coda to them, and the braking function of the coda.

Another interesting rondo is the one from Haydn's little Trio in G major for piano, violin, and violoncello. The last movement of this Trio is the well-known "Gipsy Rondo" ("Rondo all'ongarese").

Before we continue our analysis let us note that capital letters will be used in our diagrams for sections, small letters for subsections.

This is a rondo with five sections. Haydn uses section *A* as a kind of unifying frame; between statements of it he can introduce several gypsy dance strains. Section *A* is a small ternary form:

The return to subsection *a* will be obvious to the listener.
What may not be clear, however, is the device that Haydn
uses to extend this small ternary form. He does it by repeat-
ing the first *a* and following this by a repetition of *ba*. The
listener hears this extension of the fundamental *aba* scheme
as *aababa*. Its relation to the ternary form may be seen from
the way Haydn used repeat marks:

$$\|{:}\quad a \quad {:}\|{:}\quad b\ a\quad {:}\|$$

The listener is often asked to accept this conventional device as an amplification of a small ternary structure.

With section *B* begins the introduction of characteristic
gypsy tunes and rhythms. There are four of them, each repeated:

Section *A* returns, this time without repeats.

Section *C* introduces two more gypsy tunes, both of them
in minor, on the same key level as the beginning of the
piece:

Notice that both these gypsy tunes have the following syncopated rhythmic motive:

At the end of the final appearance of section *A*, Haydn needs a coda. Notice how he leads to it with this figure, which is the main theme in a version turned upside down:

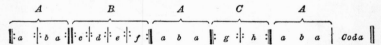

Notice, too, how he gradually puts on the brakes in the coda as he brings the music to a satisfactory ending.

This sprightly rondo is remarkable for the large number of different motives Haydn has been able to set at ease within the confines of a short piece of music. A chart of the form will show what he has done:

          A   *B*   *A*   *C*   *A*

‖: a :‖: b a :‖‖: c :‖: d :‖: e :‖: f :‖ a b a ‖: g :‖: h :‖ a b a | *Coda* ‖

By now the listener should know about what to expect from a rondo, at least when he knows ahead of time that the music is in rondo form. If he doesn't know ahead of time he can hear the music again—music is intended for more than one hearing! Rondos are fun, and no music lover could object to hearing more. Beethoven used the form twice in the sonata for piano, Op. 13, that is known as the "Sonata Pathétique." The second and third movements are both in rondo form.

A sketch will serve to guide the listener through the second movement of the "Pathétique." As he listens, however, he can afford to give attention to all of the materials out of which Beethoven has made this music:

A

Melody stated twice, the second time an octave higher

B

Notice the passage that leads back to *A*.

A

Melody stated once

C

Notice how the forward motion in the accompaniment turns to triplets.

A

Notice the passage that leads to this reiteration of *A*, and how the triplet motion continues under the melody.

Coda

The coda grows out of the triplet motion which continued through the last *A* from section *C*. The melodic line is related to the motive which appeared in the bass of section *C*.

Now let the listener try himself on the final movement of the "Sonata Pathétique." It moves so rapidly that it can take in a good deal of thematic material. Section *A* begins with the most important melodic line of the movement. Notice that it is in minor:

A bridge passage leads from section *A* to section *B*, which contains two contrasting subjects:

Section *A* returns with its original thematic material. Then we hear section *C*, based on a theme in half-notes:

Notice how this theme moves from the top to the bottom of the music, how it is syncopated and then given a rapid accompaniment. A bridge passage leads back to section *A*. This time, part of the melodic line is heard underneath the accompaniment.

So far we have heard five parts of a rondo form, but Beethoven does not stop there. He goes on to another section, but instead of introducing new thematic material he uses again the material of section *B*. This double appearance of section *B* is perhaps the reason for its two themes. A bridge leads from the second appearance of section *B* to another *A*, which is short and leads directly to the coda. The coda ends with a precipitous scale and heavy chord, but this ending is preceded by a quiet reminiscence of the most important melodic motive:

In following this Beethoven music the listener must learn to make a distinction between two functions of the melodic line. The longer and more complex a piece of music is, the more careful the composer must be to secure a smooth transition from one section to the next. As a result of this necessity the melodic line must at times carry the melodic motives and at other times make the transitions. For the listener this entails distinguishing between the places where the melodic line is really saying something and where it is simply moving toward a point where it will again have important subject matter. A feeling for this motion toward a goal is not difficult to cultivate, especially in listening to the Beethoven piece we are discussing. The passage leading to the coda is a good example. A motive that has been connected with the main theme suddenly melts into a long passage of rapid notes:

The careful listener to this rondo will discover that Beethoven uses a special short motive only for transitions. See how often you can find it:

The last movement of Beethoven's "Sonata Pathétique" is, then, a rondo with seven sections. The plan is as follows:

A⌢B⌢A⌢C⌢A⌢B⌢A⌢Coda

The rondo is an interesting form. As an extension of the fundamental principle of repetition after contrast, it may be exceedingly simple or complex. Knowing it, we not only have a guide to a great deal of music, but we have made considerable progress toward understanding the logic of musical architecture.

RECORDINGS

Schubert	*Rosamunde:* Entr'acte	Victor 6673-B
Haydn	Trio in G major: "Rondo all'ongarese"	Victor 3046-B
Beethoven	"Sonata Pathétique," Op. 13: Adagio cantabile; Rondo	Victor 6772

Chapter 11

THE MINUET

SOME of the oldest of the conventional musical forms developed out of the practical considerations surrounding the making of dance music. As the rhythmic and melodic characteristics of dance music came to the attention of composers—and this happened a long time ago—the forms also attracted interest. At the time when the forms of much of the music we know today were crystallizing, the minuet was the fashionable ballroom dance. It was natural that composers should adopt the minuet, with its characteristic rhythm and form, as one of the movements of the sonata and the symphony.

The minuet, as a dance, invariably in three-four time, was slow and stately. As a concert piece, it has retained the three-four time, but not always the slow and stately movement. Just as it would be difficult to use Gershwin's "Rhapsody in Blue" for ballroom dancing, although its derivation from jazz and its consequent relation to dancing are obvious, so it would be difficult to dance the minuet of tradition to the music that appears on concert programs as minuets. The general outlines of the old minuet, however, have been retained for our conventional form, although for concert music it has not been necessary to adhere to the precise number of measures that would fit the figures of the dance.

Looking at the printed score of a minuet would show that the music has two distinct sections; it would look almost like two separate pieces of music, the first labeled minuet; the second, trio. The use of the word "trio" in this connection comes from the fact that the whole ballroom orchestra played the minuet proper but only three instruments were used in the trio. That tradition remains only in the use of the word and the fact that the trio is often either more lightly orchestrated or narrower in texture than the minuet.

That the score looks as if it splits into two pieces is deceiving. At the end of the trio the composer writes "Minuet da capo" (D.C.), and this instructs the performers to return to the beginning and play the minuet proper again. Consequently, in general outline, the minuet form as a whole is ternary:

$$A \qquad\qquad B \qquad\qquad A$$
$$\text{Minuet} \qquad\quad \text{Trio} \qquad\quad \text{Minuet}$$

But each section in itself is also a ternary form. The first two have, moreover, the kind of repeats that we found at the beginning of the Haydn "Gipsy Rondo":

$$\|: a :\|: b \ a :\|$$

At the return of the minuet, these repeats are omitted.

The minuet, then, may be called a compound ternary form, and a diagram of it needs to show the internal shape of each section:

$$\overbrace{\|:a \quad :\|: b \quad a \quad :\|}^{\substack{A \\ \text{Minuet}}} \overbrace{\|:c \quad :\|: d \quad c \quad :\|}^{\substack{B \\ \text{Trio}}} \overbrace{\|a \quad\quad b \quad\quad a \quad \|}^{\substack{A \\ \text{Minuet}}}$$

One other characteristic of the minuet must be mentioned. The trio is invariably in a different key from the minuet. If the minuet begins in major the trio will usually be in the key of the dominant; if the minuet is in minor the trio will be either in the relative major or in the major on the same tonic.[1] This means that the minuet must have either an ending that will lead in two directions—back to make the repeat or on to the trio—or it must have two endings. Such, by the way, is the reason for endings that differ, wherever they may be found.

With this guide to the minuet in mind or with the book open to the chart, let us listen to some minuets. An excellent one with which to begin is the Minuet from Mozart's String Quartet in D minor (K.V. 421).

The melodic line of both subsections *a* and *b* of the minuet proper grows out of a motive that is really more rhythmic than melodic, a kind of motto:

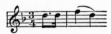

In the first subsection it is used as part of the melodic motive:

In the second subsection it has this appearance:

The minuet proper is so closely wrought that the texture is really polyphonic. The use of the three-note motive to give melodic interest to the parts of all the instruments deserves complete hearing. The music is so delightful and so characteristic of Mozart that the score of the first short part is given here.

---

[1] This terminology sounds complex. All the terms used have been explained in former chapters or in the Appendix. The important thing to hear, however, is the fact that a change occurs in level or mode—in key or as between major and minor—or in both.

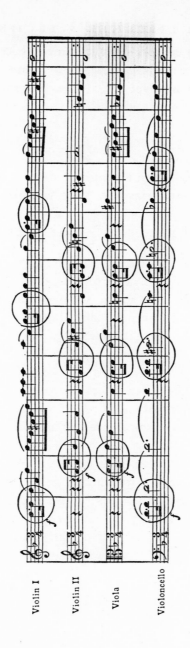

The trio is in major, on the same tonic as the minuet. Here again the melodic line for both subsections grows out of a very short motive: ♪♩. The first subsection begins with this melodic line, played by the first violin:

In the second subsection the motive develops into a different melodic line, characterized by very wide leaps:

The texture of the trio, in contrast to that of the minuet proper, is monophonic. The melodic line demands most of the listener's attention; the accompaniment consists only of very simple plucked or pizzicato chords. The return of the minuet, without internal repetitions, brings the music to a close.

After the listener has heard this minuet several times he will be as much impressed by its compactness as by its sound. Before we go on to other illustrations of the minuet form we may profitably discuss some of the implications of this compactness.

First, the kind of close-knit quality that this music exhibits is an aspect of the melodic and rhythmic style of the piece. We may decide, indeed, as we become familiar with more of Mozart's music, that it is characteristic of his general style. This quality grows directly out of the fact that only two identifying motives are used. Stripped of all appended melodic qualities, the minuet proper is a musical discussion of this motive: ♩.♪ | ♩. The trio is even more strikingly fashioned from one small motive: ♪♩. These two motives, moreover, have a distinct relationship to each other. The second is simply a rhythmic reversal of the first two notes of the first.

♪. ♩ reversed, is ♪♩.

Composers make use of such relationships of mirrorlike reversal time after time, with the expectation that the listener will have no more difficulty than in recognizing a photographic negative. Actually, then, Mozart made this piece out of *tum te dum* (♪.♩♩).

Aside from its admirable craftsmanship, what does this compactness imply? What does it imply that will help the listener hear music? The implication is important to our understanding of musical form.

We must return, for the moment, to our diagram of the minuet form:

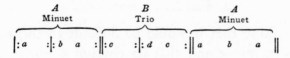

If this form were only a mold into which the composer poured as much music as he could, it would have room for four distinct musical ideas represented by the letters *a, b, c,* and *d.* But composers do not always use a form to unify as many ideas as possible, as Haydn did in the "Gipsy Rondo." Often they use it rather to give variety of treatment to a single idea. An important distinction is to be noted between unifying many ideas and giving variety of treatment to one idea. These two functions of form are met with *wherever ideas take form.* It might even be suggested that ideas do not exist until they have form.

Mozart, in the minuet from which all this is a digression more apparent than real, is giving form to one idea. *Tum te dum* is not an idea but rather a motto or text. The letters in our diagram will correspond, for this piece, not to points at which new ideas are introduced, but stages in the musical discussion which, in a verbal treatment, might be marked off by "moreover," "however," or "on the other hand."

The difficulty for the listener is to get the slight distinctions in musical treatment which mark the "moreover" or the "however." It is by those distinctions that he may keep his place in the music. Let us practice with another Mozart minuet, the famous one from the Symphony No. 40 in G minor.

For *a* in the minuet proper, Mozart immediately states his most important musical idea:

It is so striking that it would be difficult to forget. Notice that it is in minor and that its rhythm conflicts with the basic three-four measure of the minuet. It could be written more comfortably in a two-four measure:

When Mozart gets to the "however" marked by the *b* on our diagram he makes his point by emphasizing even more strongly the syncopation of this subject theme. To accomplish this, the theme at *b* is characterized by a strong dissonance on the down beat, a beat normally lost under the syncopation. The listener must feel the bite of this dissonance and how its quality continues in the musical discussion:

flute, oboes,
viola, violoncello

violins
bassoons

At *b,* too, the subject has momentarily gone into the relative major. Thus the position of *b* in the form is marked not by a new melodic motive, but by a new treatment of the original motive.

The return of *a* (after *b*) is not a mechanical repetition of the beginning of the piece, as it might be and as it actually is in many minuets, but, with less space, different tone-color, and new harmony, a return, in the flute, of the original *minor* form of the motive. Notice the descending chromatic notes in the bassoon part at this point.

The trio introduces another motive. Its relation to the subject of the minuet proper is perhaps a little remote, but it can be shown by putting one above the other and comparing the melodic contour.

Minuet

Trio

The four eighth notes which appear after two statements of the trio motive are similar to the eighth notes in the minuet subject:

Minuet

Trio

The trio, then, has a kind of "on the other hand" relation to the minuet proper. Its tone-color is in complete contrast, and its key is G major, the tonic major of G minor. Here, as in the minuet, the same motive is the motto for both parts of the form:

The return of *c*, like the return of *a* in the minuet proper, is not a literal repetition. The French horns are added to the violin statement of the motive, and its second statement is piled up with a polyphonic imitation by the French horns and woodwinds.

This Mozart minuet, one of the most interesting in all symphonic literature, deserves many hearings. It will well repay, in musical understanding, a close attempt to *hear* what has been outlined in this discussion. To aid in this hearing, a full score of this minuet has been included at the end of this chapter. When the listener can close this book and trace in his listening *all* the things that Mozart makes this music do, he has made real progress in the language of music.

The minuet form has been presented as a conventional musical structure; yet the examples used have been unconventional minuets. A conventional minuet, if it could be found—one that made the process of illustrating the form easy—would convey an entirely false impression of the delightful variety of minuets. The listener must learn to take music as it comes from the hand of the composer, even though it varies from the textbook form. Form and idea or content are not to be separated except as an aid in learning.

The experienced listener will invariably give his most ardent admiration to music which, for a reason, departs even radically from the imaginary norm. With only a few hints as to what the listener may find, let us hear another minuet, this time one by Schubert, from his String Quartet in A minor, Op. 29. Play it. Notice first how Schubert uses the little motive that Mozart used in the first minuet we heard:

More than from his use of the motive, however, the pure magic of this minuet results from Schubert's avoidance of the conventional key relations of the form. The listener is actually left up in the air until near the end of the second *a* in the minuet proper. The violoncello begins the second *a* clearly enough, but after it has reiterated the motive several times it slides off into a completely strange key. Why? The answer must be found in what the music does to arrive finally at the long organ point which tells us that the harmony has come home. Listen for the magnificent *harmonic*

forward motion that is outlined by the violoncello. Here is the richness of chromaticism. Try to hum the 'cello part from the return to *a* to the trio.

$$|:a \quad :|:b \quad \underline{a \quad :|}$$

hum the
'cello part
here

Notice in the trio how the original motive is used to make the change to major. But then try to decide on the form of the trio. The lack of definiteness which, in the minuet proper, appeared in harmonic relations, affects form and melody in the trio.

With these hints, study this minuet for yourself. You will find that it is a remarkable piece of music. It is interesting partly because it represents a great genius's departure from a conventional form for the sake of what he had to say.

Musical form is a guide, a map, for the listener. In that function, however, it must be used as much to determine departure from the conventional norm as conformity to it. This has been true of the rondo and the minuet. It will be even truer of the sonata.

RECORDINGS

Mozart	String Quartet in D minor (K.V. 421): Minuet	Victor 7608
	Symphony No. 40: Minuet	Victor 8885
Schubert	String Quartet in A minor, Op. 29: Minuet	Victor 11718

138

Menuetto da capo

Chapter 12

THE SONATA FORM

MANY listeners have been puzzled by the word "sonata" because it has so many meanings in current usage among musicians. An explanation which will clarify those meanings will be of value as we proceed.

At almost exactly the same time that our English forefathers were planting colonies on this continent—the first third of the seventeenth century—musicians in Europe were discovering that music for instruments could be different in style from music for voices. They had been playing the same music they sang. For the new market which was created by the growing number of instrumentalists—amateurs like Samuel Pepys, for example—printers, with the connivance of composers, began to announce on title pages that pieces were "apt for voices or viols." In Italy the expression was "per cantare o suonare." But as the style of writing for instruments began to differentiate, composers discovered that they could write passages for instruments (*per suonare*) that were not suitable for voices (*per cantare*). As this difference became more and more obvious even the publishers had to recognize it. Composers and printers alike fell into the custom of calling a piece that was intended to be sung a *cantata,* and a piece to be played—a piece of instrumental music—a *sonata.* Since the beginning of the seventeenth century people have called single pieces of instrumental music by so many other names that this first use of the word "sonata" has all but disappeared. Occasionally, however, pianists and, more recently, harpsichordists play some of the sonatas of Domenico Scarlatti, which are rather short single pieces. Thus the word still has some slight currency with this early meaning.

Composers very soon began to compose groups of pieces, with the intention that all the pieces be played in sequence, and they called these groups of pieces sonatas. From this practice we get our common meaning of the word: a group of movements which somehow belong together. Two considerably different uses appeared for the sonatas of this early period. Out of each use a style developed, and for each style a modification of the name was applied. Thus a group of instrumental pieces of a style proper to church use was called a *sonata da chiesa* or church sonata. A group of less serious, more amusing pieces, characteristically containing several dances, was called a *sonata da camera* or living-room sonata. This, by the way, is the source of our expression "chamber music."

The story at this point, to be accurate, would have to be too complex for our present purpose. It is sufficient to note that *suites, lessons, partitas*, and *ordres* were groups of pieces which, had they been composed in Italy, probably would all have been called sonatas.

Our concert and radio programs and the shelves of record dealers often make sonatas of this second type available to modern listeners. The sonatas, suites, and partitas of composers like Bach, Handel, Corelli, and many others give this meaning currency.

During the eighteenth century, styles in music, like styles

in everything from manners to government, underwent a radical change. And just as a change in the style of government brought with it new governmental forms, so a change in musical style made necessary new musical forms. Composers wanted to continue composing groups of movements which gave them a sonata of adequately large dimensions, but they had to have new forms for the movements of the sonata. The problem was particularly acute with regard to long, rapid movements. The form, then, that was devised for the individual movements of the sonata, particularly the first, came to be called the sonata form.

We have, in consequence, the following uses for the word *sonata*:

1. A name for a single piece of instrumental music.
2. A name for a group of movements.
3. A name for a form for single movements within a group.

Some sonatas include movements in sonata form; some do not. The matter is further complicated. A symphony is really a sonata for symphony orchestra; a string quartet is a sonata for two violins, viola, and violoncello; a trio for piano, violin, and violoncello is a sonata for those three instruments. Operatic overtures composed since the sonata form developed are often in sonata form. The sonata form is heard more often than any other. The complications of its history and use drop out of sight when the form becomes familiar. But the listener must not look for it where it could not possibly be, as, for instance, in the pieces and groups of pieces called sonatas that were composed before the sonata form was invented.

The sonata form is a form for one single movement. What is it like?

In the scale of complexity, as in the scale of value as a vehicle for great music, it is at the top of the group of forms which have grown out of the application of the basic principle of repetition after contrast. Its main outline, from the standpoint of the listener, is ternary:

A   B   A

Each section exhibits a characteristic inner organization which is implied in the name given to that section. The first or *A* section is the *exposition*. The *B* section is the *development*. The second *A* is the *recapitulation*.

A   B   A
Exposition   Development   Recapitulation

Each of these words describes the function of the section to which it is applied. In the exposition the composer states the subject matter for the movement. In the development he explores and discusses the implications of the subject matter. In the recapitulation he restates the original subject matter and brings the movement to a close.

The formal organization within the exposition allows for the introduction not only of contrasting thematic material but of change in key. It begins with a *first theme* which not only presents the first musical subject matter but establishes the key. The contrasting section which follows states the *second theme*. The second theme is in a new key, and because the arrival of both the new theme and the new key requires preparation, the first theme and the second are connected by a *bridge passage*. The bridge may be accorded greater or less space and emphasis, depending on the requirements of the particular piece of music; it is, however, always a passage in which the motion from one theme and key to another should be obvious to the listener. This first bridge, too, has another significance, which will appear in relation to the recapitulation. The exposition ends with a *closing episode* which may introduce either new subject matter or a different form of any earlier thematic material. When it is time to leave the second theme and move to the closing episode, another bridge provides passage to the latter. The closing episode is, however, conventionally in the same key as the second theme.

The composers who first conceived the sonata form habitually indicated that the entire exposition was to be repeated in performance. Modern performers use their own taste and judgment about making the repeats. If the repeat is made, the music must shift from the key of the second theme back to that of the first theme. If the repeat is omitted or after it has been made, the music must move on to the development. Thus the final measures of the exposition must be so fashioned that they will lead in either one of two directions.

The traditional sonata form also establishes the exact key relationship between the themes. If the first theme is in major, the second theme is on the level of the dominant. If the first theme is in minor, the second theme is in the relative major. The exposition ends, naturally, in the key of the second theme. All this is rather complex; it is, moreover, a tradition which composers themselves often find reason for breaking. For the listener who is struggling to understand the sonata form it is sufficient at the beginning to try to feel the movement away from one level toward the establishment of the new level. This is not difficult.

A diagram for the exposition looks like this:

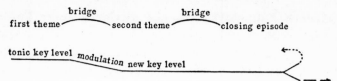

The development section of the sonata form has no conventional pattern. This fact, on first thought, may appear to leave the listener without guidance for part of the music. Although no aspect of the sonata form can be described without making a reservation for possible exceptions, the development is almost certain to be based on material which is familiar from having been presented in the exposition. While there is no set form for the development, at least its very nature stipulates its subject matter. The listener who has really *heard* the exposition will find satisfaction, as his experience with music increases, in the composer's having been left free in the development to follow the bent of his own originality. Most music composed in this most monumental of musical forms is worth hearing many times. As the listener begins to live with his favorite sonata-form music, he will find that each development section has its own inevitable structure. This individual form is a logical projection from the exposition and grows out of the implications of the subject matter. Those implications will usually include considerable change of key. The piling up of intensity as the music proceeds makes the tension which may result from rapid modulation more valuable here than at any other point in the sonata. The development can be the most thrilling part of the music. As it comes to a close it returns to the key level on which the exposition began.

The recapitulation follows the general outline of the exposition with two important differences. Composers have learned, after long experience, that the sense of completeness, of inevitability, which they wish to convey in a piece of music, depends to a considerable extent upon the emphasis given at the end of the piece to the key level of the beginning. This is especially true of the sonata, where the development permits so much fluctuation. Here repetition after contrast is vital. We have seen, in our study of theme and variations, the care with which Haydn and Schubert, by means of an organ point, emphasized the return to the tonic after chromatic or modulatory excursions in the previous variation. In the recapitulation in the sonata form this increased emphasis is secured by keeping all of the section on the key level of the first theme. As a result, the bridge between the first and second themes must end where it began. The passage which was heard partly as a shift in key level in the exposition takes on a novel sound and often has different length and importance in the recapitulation. This is the first important difference between the exposition and the recapitulation.

The second difference also grows out of the fact that the music must finally come to an end. Neither of the endings of the exposition, both of which led toward a continuation, could be satisfactory endings for the whole movement. They usually go in the wrong direction harmonically, and they are not long enough in relation to the momentum that the movement has gathered. All this means that the recapitulation must end in a coda; it may consist either of a different final turn to the closing episode or of an addition to it.

One other detail of the sonata form must be noted. The sonatas which were written before the change of style that necessitated the invention of the sonata form often began with a comparatively short slow movement. Such a slow

The Sonata Form

Introduction
(may or may not be present)

A
Exposition

first theme · bridge · second theme · bridge · closing episode

repeat may occur here

B
Development

A
Recapitulation

first theme · bridge · second theme · bridge · closing episode · Coda

Key level

movement did not continue as an integral part of the new sonata form, but it furnished a tradition for a slow introduction to the movement which was to be in sonata form. A slow introduction precedes the movement in sonata form only when the composer has a particular reason for using it. Some sonatas have it; others do not. One of the most interesting sources of insight for the listener may be speculation as to why a composer uses or omits a slow introduction.

We are ready for a diagram of the entire sonata form. It will be a diagram which, even more than that of the rondo, must be looked upon as a guide in cases of both conformity and nonconformity. Music would be a poor thing indeed if composers were forced by law to conform to a convention.

The foregoing description of the sonata form is too long to make interesting reading. Hearing a sonata, however, may become a fascinating musical experience, and it would be unfair to deny the listener any of the information which makes real hearing possible. Do not try to use a description of music like this as light reading. No one ever yet read himself into an understanding of music, any more than a prospective airplane pilot reads himself into a pilot's license—*that takes hours in the air*. With music, intelligent mastery takes hours *with the music*. This description must be used as a manual. Reference to it should be continued until the listener knows the sonata form well enough to be able to refer to it from memory.

Experience with music which uses the sonata form will make the form itself much more intelligible. We must now accumulate some of our hours with the music.

Chapter 13

HEARING SONATAS

NO composer has excelled Mozart in the sheer perfection with which he used the sonata form. For him it was the perfect vehicle. Because it grew out of the musical language that he spoke, he used it time after time with no reservation as to its suitability. To observe the sonata-form structure and to feel the real simplicity of its logic, we can do no better than to turn to Mozart.

We have made the acquaintance of the Minuet from Mozart's Symphony in G minor. We will use the rest of that symphony for practice in hearing the sonata form. Let us turn, then, to the first movement of this symphony.

For the first hearing do not try to grasp too much detail. The outlines of the form as they are made clear in the subject matter must be recognized first; later hearings will fill in the details. Try to hear at least this much the first time:

[NO INTRODUCTION]

EXPOSITION

First theme grows out of this motive:

Bridge passage. First theme motive disappears. Momentary chromatic harmonies prepare for the new key—major.

A short pause announces the arrival of the second theme. Try to hear an extra theme which Mozart uses in this bridge passage. It will have considerable importance later:

Second theme. Melodic line is divided between strings and woodwinds. The theme is this:

Notice that the second theme is slightly chromatic.

Bridge passage. The melodic line of the second theme is replaced by chromatic chords and rapid notes.

Closing episode. An echoing use, between oboe and bassoon, of the motive from the first theme:

This is followed by scale passages and reiterated dominant-tonic chords; *sol-do* is heard at the bottom of the music.

Repeat of exposition. Notice that the key of the beginning is prepared for by one loud chord at the very end of the exposition. This quick dive back into the original key is not hard to *feel*. The exposition of this movement is almost invariably repeated in performance. Notice how, after the one loud chord which took the music back to the beginning, two more chords take it away from its home level for the development.

DEVELOPMENT

Follow the use of the motive: . Notice the rapid shifts in key level. Notice, too, the gentle chromatic fall back to the key of the first theme and how the first theme arrives a moment before this can be completed.

RECAPITULATION

First theme. Try to hear that the last part of the theme is here stated differently in harmony from its first presentation in the exposition. It consequently moves over slightly different intervals from those used before. It is already preparing for the second theme's re-location as to key level which is characteristic of the recapitulation.

Bridge passage. This is much longer and more important than the corresponding passage in the exposition. Try to hear the rather extended treatment of the little surprise theme that was noticed in the exposition:

Try to hear how Mozart piles up the last four notes in an imitation between the first violins and the violas, violoncellos, and bassoons:

Second theme. After a long bridge passage the second theme enters as it did before. Try to hear, if from nothing else than the quality of its sound, that it is on a lower key level than in the exposition.

Bridge passage. The same, except for key level, as in the exposition.

Closing episode. The same, except for key level and ending, as in the exposition. Notice that it leads to the coda by a chromatically ascending syncopated passage:

Coda. This brings back the material of the first theme, but with an imitative treatment:

Notice how the first violin continues with what is designated here as *b*, and how it is imitated in turn by the viola. In the final ending, notice the use of the rhythm of the first theme, with the long insistence on the dominant-tonic or *do-sol* harmonies.

If this sketch is not clear after one or two hearings, try listening to the music while you keep your place on the map on page 155.

As the listener's acquaintance with music grows, he will find that a sketch of the form which will help him to keep from getting lost serves only as a clue to the true character of the music. As he penetrates the movement under discus-

First Movement, Mozart's G minor Symphony

Exposition

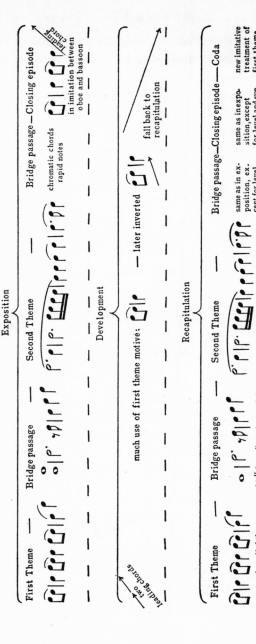

First Theme — **Bridge passage** — **Second Theme** — **Bridge passage** — **Closing episode**

First Theme: passage has slightly different ending

Bridge passage: this "theme" much extended. Last four notes in imitation (as in a round) ends on a different level

Second Theme: same level as first theme, which is a

Bridge passage: chromatic chords rapid notes

Closing episode: in imitation between oboe and bassoon

leading chord

Development

much use of first theme motive: — later inverted

two leading chords

fall back to recapitulation

Recapitulation

First Theme — **Bridge passage** — **Second Theme** — **Bridge passage** — **Closing episode** — **Coda**

Bridge passage: this "theme" much extended. Last four notes in imitation (as in a round) ends on a different level

Second Theme: same level as first theme, which is a new level for this theme.

Bridge passage: same as in exposition, except for level

Closing episode: same as in exposition, except for level and syncopated, chromatic lead into coda

Coda: new imitative treatment of first theme motive.

sion it should continue to grow on him, not only until its form seems clear and logical, but until hearing it becomes a unified living experience.

Is there any relationship, for instance, among the following qualities of this music? Both first and second themes emphasize a quality of melodic motion that is rather gentle. The listener may choose, with perfect justice, other adjectives to describe them; he must be sure, however, that they fit what the music does. Aside from all differences in actual motive material, these two themes have a *quality* in common. The first theme presses forward with more insistence than the second; the second has a tentative, suspended quality as a result of the fact that it postpones the arrival of the clear tonic harmony until the final note of its second phrase:

Try to hear that suspended quality. Compare it with the long tonic harmony at the beginning of the first theme. There is considerable difference in *degree* between the two themes, but they do have a graceful, gentle quality in common.

Compare that quality with the force—tremendous by contrast—of the momentary theme of the bridge passage between them in the exposition:

Notice, too, that once in the statement of the first theme Mozart has hammered on the plain rhythmic aspect of the motive:

Then consider the momentary strength of the dive which returns the music to the beginning and then takes it on to the development. These almost hidden qualities of strength contrast with the main themes. What happens to them as the music proceeds?

There can be little question concerning the development. Although it ends with a graceful and gentle dropping back to the first theme in the recapitulation, it has devoted its whole space to adding vitality, strength, and force to the first theme. Notice its rhythmic and harmonic energy and the power of its climax even within the limited orchestra Mozart employs—no kettledrums, no trumpets, no trombones. Then, above all, feel the effect of the remarkable development of the bridge passage in the recapitulation. It is as if the hidden strength of the exposition, beginning to appear in the development, now finds justification for a burst of exuberance. And finally, after a rather wistful beginning, the coda hammers at the rhythmic strength of the first theme:

And it ends with a display of what most listeners and composers will always feel to be the most tremendously powerful relationship in the whole realm of musical materials, the repeated harmonic movement from dominant to tonic.

Is this a plot? Does the movement of the music *move* the listener? Does Mozart control how the listener is moved?

The sonata form is a form for experience!

The final movement of the same symphony is another opportunity for insight. Our discussion, as we proceed, may depend more and more upon the listener's growing understanding of musical language. The sketch of this movement on page 160 should be sufficient. Here the music has a compactness which is apt to characterize the final movements of symphonies, and the exposition is seldom repeated in performance.

Notice that the first theme is actually a small ternary structure, with its parts repeated in the convention of the minuet:

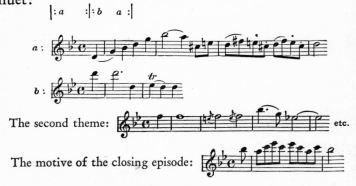

Although the sonata form was developed primarily for the rapid first movement, it has sometimes been used in slow movements. This is the case with Mozart's G minor Symphony. The slow movement shows a slightly different use of the form. Because of its leisurely pace the subject matter may be more complex. The sketch on page 161 will indicate the outlines of this movement. Here are the themes:

First theme:

Second theme:

Closing episode:

The intricacies of this slow movement, which flows past the listener with such seeming lack of complexity, will respond to several hearings, and the movement will become as clear as any of the others.

The reader who has been following this book with some care should now be reminded that he has acquainted himself with all of Mozart's Symphony in G minor. He owes it to himself and to Mozart to hear the movements in the order which the composer intended. Notice that the second movement is in a different key from the others. Play them now straight through in turn. This symphony is a great masterpiece. If you now can hear it well enough so that it takes shape in your mind—so that it has a distinct personality of its own—you are learning the language of music.

RECORDING

Mozart   Symphony No. 40 in G minor (K.V. 550)   Victor M-293

Last Movement (Finale), Mozart's G minor Symphony

Exposition

First Theme — Bridge passage — Second Theme — Bridge passage — Closing episode

First Theme

a | :‖ *b* *a* :‖   etc.

Bridge passage

thematic material derived from a

Second Theme

Bridge passage

material derived from same source as that of first bridge passage

Closing episode

Development

Based almost entirely on material of the first theme; notice modulations, polyphonic treatment of thematic material

Return to key of first theme

Recapitulation

First Theme — Bridge passage — Second Theme — Bridge passage — Closing episode Coda

First Theme

shorter than in the exposition

| *a* *b* *a* |

Bridge passage

leads to normal second theme key, no extension

Second Theme

slightly longer than in the exposition. Notice the emphasis on its chromatic character.

Bridge passage

same as in the exposition except for level

Closing episode Coda

Second (Slow) Movement, Mozart's G minor Symphony

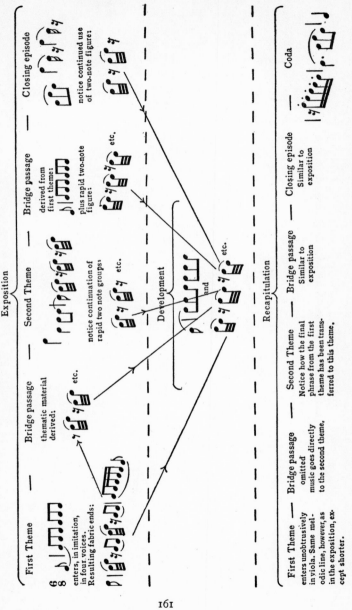

Part Two

MUSIC AS LITERATURE

Chapter 14

MUSIC IS LITERATURE

HENRY ADAMS, in *The Education of Henry Adams,* an autobiography in which the sole interest is in the growth of its author in his relation to *ideas,* devotes a short passage to the beginning of his education as a listener. That passage contains two interesting phrases. After telling how bored he had been with music, Adams related his great surprise when he discovered that music could form a "pattern in his mind." In describing his astonishment he says that "it was as if a curtain had been raised upon a new sense." This from a Bostonian who had been hearing music all his life!

If the first part of this book has succeeded only partially, the listener must have felt music becoming a pattern in his mind. Perhaps his astonishment was not remarkable, but if a new sense, a new power, has developed with regard to music, he is making progress as a listener.

The fact that music can have the power that Adams found in it—the power that we all find in it as we begin to understand it—is sufficient support for the title of this chapter. *Music actually is thought.* One can, with equal justification, use the expressions "English thought," "German thought," "musical thought." The individual who, like Henry Adams, has an intense curiosity concerning what happens to him from the ears up, reads English or German books for their thought—for the thought of the men who wrote what he reads. Likewise he listens to music for its thought—for the thought of the men who expressed their ideas in the language of music.

One difficulty confronts us at this point. It is a difficulty largely of habit. In verbal language—and this is true even with poetry—we habitually give more attention to the meanings of the words and sentences than to the sensuous charm of the sound, which every true lover of language knows has its own musiclike significance. We follow the idea through the maze of words, phrases, sentences, paragraphs, and chapters which are necessary for its complete embodiment.

In music, on the other hand, the sensuous charm of the sound of the language too often makes the strongest appeal to our attention. We enjoy the gratification of our senses and get from such gratification as vague a meaning as we would from a strange language well spoken; but we fail to follow the musical idea through the structure in which it is embodied.

Music exerts its charm in spite of our failure to understand it, but such partial value is too much like the pleasure the old lady got from hearing her minister use the word "Mesopotamia." It leaves the intelligent person with a sense of futility. Out of that sense of futility comes, tragically, the feeling that music is not a language. The habit of not understanding music leads to the judgment that music, by its very nature, cannot be understood.

With considerable justice it can be said that the very charm of the sound of musical language may be a handicap to the perception of its meaning. Why did Beethoven, for instance—especially in his mature works—avoid lusciousness unless from the desire to focus his listeners' attention on inner meaning? This notion may seem revolutionary to many listeners. Without it, however, much music could not even be enjoyed, for its attraction is not wholly or even mostly sensuous.

The purpose of the whole first part of this book has been to give the listener the means whereby he may develop the habit of understanding music. That purpose cannot be consummated unless we are willing to look upon the desire to convey meaning, or thought, as the fundamental reason for the existence of great music and great composers.

The reasons for our interest in music, then, are the same as for our interest in any other literature. We want to know what and how men have thought. We want the minds of others to touch our own. We want to be enriched by the great minds of the world, including the great musical minds.

There is a thirst for knowing which has tremendous force even when its objects are only things and facts. But the thirst for knowing people and being known by them is much stronger. It rules our lives. It is almost strong enough to break through the mask we wear—the front that protects us from the fear that when we are known we will be disliked. But not quite, because that mask is a negative expression of the same essential thirst. For this reason we know only a very few of those whom we meet face to face. We feel that we are known by a similar few. Free, open, true contact of minds is rare indeed. In the sorrow that we so often feel at our failures in our relationships with others we say, "If I had only known"—and almost always our concern is for one whom we have, in some meager fashion, known for years.

The loneliness of human beings is usually felt more strongly by creative artists than by others; it is, nevertheless, normal to all of us. This feeling of loneliness, this craving to be understood, provides a powerful motive for self-expression. By expressing and communicating his ideas and feelings, the artist, whether musician, writer, or painter, diminishes his own loneliness.

Thought does not exist entirely by itself. It is accompanied by a state of feeling, by a constant flow of emotion. Homer W. Smith, in *Kamongo*, gives a vivid description of the source of this emotional flow:

Your cave-man is the key to the whole question. Without him we would be lost, but with him we can find our way. You have to understand that brain of his.

His brain worked in a quite simple fashion. On one side, so to speak, there was a storehouse where he could keep the sensory pictures—sights, smells, sounds, touch—of the world about him, and on the other there was a delivery room where he could send out orders to his muscles for action; in the middle there was a clearing-house where he could sort everything out and size it up. All his life this brain of his was busy collecting sensory information in the one side, correlating that information in the clearing-house, and acting upon the final product in the other. When he saw a mango, he ate it; when he saw a stick, he passed it by; but when he saw a mammoth, he ran!

But there was yet another part of his brain, a fourth part which we can call his emotional sounding-board. It was just as important as the other three. Whenever any sensory picture came to his brain it passed, on its way to the clearing-house, across this sounding-board where it evoked some typical emotional reaction which was itself delivered to the clearing-house simultaneously with the original sensory picture. Thus the final sensory image consisted of a picture of the object coloured by the man's emotional reaction to the object. The mango evoked in him a sensation of delight mingled, perhaps, with hunger pains and a desire to have it; the stick produced no emotional response, while the mammoth filled him with awe and fear. He did not see hunger pains in the mango or awe and fear in the mammoth—these sensations were born entirely within him by resonance from his emotional sounding-board at the base of his brain. Yet, to him, they were just as real and just as much a part of the picture as the colour and size of the mango or the length of the mammoth's tusks.

That sounding-board was a very old part of his brain. The general pattern of it had been laid down in his ancestors back in by-gone ages. So, also, had its motor connexions, and for this reason the general emotional pattern and the typical emotional responses were much the same in all men, and relatively invariable. But the specific connexions between the sounding-board and the sensory paths to his brain were mostly left unattached, so that each man was free to plug them in with the sensory pictures from the world about him according to his individual experience. As his experience widened, more and more objects came to evoke some typical emotional response, and he came to classify the world more or less in terms of his emotional reactions: good things and bad things, pleasant and unpleasant, beautiful and ugly, indifferent and awful.

That sounding-board played a very important part in his life. Its purpose was to reinforce the cold sensory image, to make it more vivid and to give it some personal, sensual colour; to give outside things a purpose, a meaning in his eyes. To meet his need it put delight in the mango; to meet his danger it put awe in the mammoth. It made the world significant—for himself.

This "sounding-board," with its long-established motor connections which control emotional responses, is the area of the mind to which music makes its appeal. As our discussion continues, the relationship between music and that sounding-board will emerge.

We may return for a moment to the suggestion that was made in a previous chapter that great music is composed by men who have qualities of greatness. In the light of our present discussion, it may be said that music gives the listener, if he understands its language, an opportunity to have a free, open, and true contact with the mind which has expressed itself in the music. Music cannot tell an untruth about the man who wrote it: it may be bad music, it may be dishonest, but in its badness or dishonesty it must tell the truth about its composer.

For music to furnish a complete experience the listener must have felt it communicating to him within its special province. It is a quality of music which the listener has to know from his emotions. Review, for a moment, your experience with the first movement of Mozart's G minor Symphony. Is it not true that when you perceived that Mozart was interested more in the *qualities* of his thematic material than in the material itself, that the growth of vitality and strength was the *point* of the movement—is it not true that then, and not until then, you felt you were beginning to understand this music?

The sheer beauty of musical sounds is the initial attraction which music offers the listener. The opportunity to search for and finally understand the meaning of music is the abiding reward. It is a reward which opens a vast storehouse of great thought, a magnificent literature.

In the search for meaning the listener needs as much guidance as in learning the obvious mechanism of the language. After he has learned to hear a piece of music completely, how is he to understand what he has heard? Unfortunately the answer is not easy, because music is a language for which words are a poor substitute. How does music talk? We can but skirt the fringes of an answer. Even a glimpse, however, will confirm us in the right to think of music as literature.

Chapter 15

HOW MUSIC TALKS

MUSIC is a source of a wide variety of experiences for the listener. Music accompanies his activities and thoughts in many different environments. He hears it in church, in the ballroom, at the theater, at the stadium, over the radio, in the restaurant, and in numberless other places. He hears it when he is in love, in sorrow; when he is studying; when he is relaxing; when he is marching; when he is worshiping. He hears it in moments of strong emotion, at times of good-fellowship and conviviality. What can it mean —how can it talk to him?

Music says what the tones do. Such a statement is clear enough, especially after we have seen how tones behave. It does not go quite far enough, however. After the listener has learned how to hear *everything* that the tones of any given piece of music do, the statement may be enlarged. *Music says what the tones do to you.* The "to you" is in effect all the time, of course, but the listener has no right to feel that there has been a complete meeting of his mind with the music while he is only partially hearing it. The sense of true meaning waits for the listener to hear the music completely.

How does this connect with what has been said earlier about the numerous contacts we have with music? In this way: Music as a background for other activities, moods, and emotions is not music at its best and highest, no matter how good the music. It supplies a way of listening that is not really listening; we do not hear all of the music—we fail to give it our complete attention. We hear only what fits our own mood at the time and thus we reverse the process by which music may be apprehended in its own meaning. In partial listening we take music into the area from which spring most of the false meanings by which the human mind is misled, the area of false association.

It cannot be denied that music has a tremendous power of associating itself with extramusical circumstances and ideas. Music, as we know it, originated because people perceived that it has such power; composers make use of it whenever they compose songs, operas, or program music. Its most modern use is on the sound track of the motion picture film. There is a subtle but very real difference, however, between true and false associations.

The listener, if he examines his own experience, will find example after example of false association. The whole of the United States, for instance, has associated intense patriotism with a tune which was originally a drinking song, "The Star-Spangled Banner." Perhaps the association is only superficially false; the lustiness of eighteenth-century conviviality may have woven a musical fabric which, when the original association has been forgotten, can be also a true reflection in music of patriotic emotion. No one has failed, at some time or other, to associate the emotion of love with some popular or even ribald song which he heard accidentally when he was deeply stirred. One may have associated an unforgettably moving incident with such a piece as "Darktown Strutters' Ball" so that the two have come to have, *by association*, the same nostalgic solemnity.

Can such associations furnish a basis for musical expression? Can a great composer depend upon them for the transmission of meaning from his mind to that of the listener? Music as literature could not exist if the answers to such questions were positive. Yet some investigators, with well-meaning diligence, have evolved numerous experiments in the attempt to measure the meaning value of exactly such associations. They might as well try to determine the meaning of words in the same way. The attempt to use such meanings is a blind-alley deduction from the supposition that music is a universal language in the sense that it need not be learned. Too many listeners go astray at exactly this point. The distinction between true and false associations must be kept in mind. True associations are possible—are sometimes indicated by the composer—and are made just often enough by pure accident so that they seemingly justify the listener who thinks he can depend upon them for the meaning of music.

One of the most prolific sources of seemingly justifiable associations is that musical sounds can be made to imitate natural sounds. The bleating of sheep and the sound of the windmill in Strauss's "Don Quixote," the thunderstorm in Beethoven's "Pastoral" Symphony, the striking of the clock in Saint-Saëns's "Danse Macabre," or the gait of the donkey in Grofé's "Grand Canyon Sketches," are a few examples among many. This possibility cannot be lightly waved aside. It has been used too often with telling effect by too many composers. Upon it, moreover, depends a great deal of the expressive power of tone-color. The determination of the truth or falsity of such associations depends upon the purpose of the composer in using them. They are, at best, a side issue in the language of music.

If associations which music can make so powerfully are not wholly to be trusted as a clue to musical meaning, in what aspect of music is meaning to be found? An answer to that question must be given by each composer for himself if his music is to justify its existence. It must be given, too, by the listener if he is to make a true contact with the composer. The answer has been given, thousands of times, by those for whom it was vital. It has been given by composers whose music talks; it has been given by listeners who have understood. But it has never been given in words so that it could be convincing.

The following attempt to furnish a verbal guide so that the listener may try to answer the question for himself must not be misunderstood. It grows out of no special claim to insight—out of no claim to have found an answer where others have failed. It grows, rather, out of the necessity of the listener's possessing, at this most crucial point in his relation to music, at least a dependable clue to what the composer puts into his music in the way of meaning. It must be practical, usable! The listener must be able to prove it in his own experience. It will, in consequence, be open to criticism from the psychologist and philosopher, to whom it will seem too simple and lacking in needle-sharpness of terminology. The listener may criticize it because it is too complex! Whatever the reaction, *it is utterly unfair to talk about music appreciation without attempting to answer the question:* HOW DOES MUSIC TALK?

We have suggested that music as literature is thought and experience plus feeling-tone or flow of emotion. If it can be shown how music, which *says* what the tones *do,* can stimulate, under the conscious direction of the composer, a flow of emotion, the answer to our question will be within reach.

Let us begin by discussing for a moment the *art* of the composer. After he has become a master of the technicalities of composition, he is ready to compose music which will convey whatever he has to express to the listener. He knows before he begins what he wants his music to say. He may know it almost subconsciously—undoubtedly has not expressed it in words—but know it he must. It is something that can be felt in an immeasurably shorter space of time than is taken by the process of composition. He cannot maintain the mood of the music within himself the whole time he is composing. He must know how to translate a complex pattern of feeling-states, which he has experienced in the past, into a piece of music. Herein consists his art. He cannot express emotion without it. We can give way to emotion, but that is not expressing it. If you see somebody in a tantrum, you will react emotionally, but hardly by reflecting the tantrum.

What is emotion? We do not want a psychologist's answer to that question. Even composers, who must arouse and direct emotion, can know psychology only in a limited way, from their own practical experience. The experience of the race, as it has crystallized in words, will give us all the clue we need. What do we mean when we say that we have had a *moving* experience; that we have been deeply *moved* or *stirred*? Is it an accident that the word which represents what we are discussing is all *motion* except the first letter: e-*motion*? The other words which actually describe how we feel all imply motion: depressed, elated, thrilled, strained, restrained, released, repressed, etc. We use such expressions as "I felt like jumping up and down" or "that stopped me in my tracks." These words and expressions, and more like them which the reader can list for himself, seem to indicate that there is a close relationship between motion and emotion. Our emotions feel to us like motions that we usually do not make. They are "pent up" even in situations for which we normally would not use that expression. We actually know our emotions to an appreciable extent through our blood pressure, viscera, and muscles—through the constant, kaleidoscopic accumulation and release of bodily tensions. It might be added, parenthetically, that the so-called lie detector is based on this relationship between emotion and bodily tension.

Emotion, then, is felt as motion.

What is music? The answer should be clear and obvious. Music is motion. Rhythm is forward motion. Melodic line is another kind of forward motion to which the possibility of pitch variation has added upward and downward motion. Harmony is forward motion for which the qualities of wideness and thinness, major and minor, rest and activity, consonance and dissonance, and diatonic and chromatic supply an immense variety of tensions. Tone-color in its most obvious aspect is not motion, but its function, aside from the associational values previously mentioned, is to clarify the lines of melodic motion. In the sense that loudness and softness are tone-color, this aspect of musical materials does supply the motion between dynamic extremes.

The conclusion toward which we are moving should be taking shape. It has been summarized by a psychologist who has long been interested in the meaning of music in the following paragraphs:

In trying to solve this ancient problem in aesthetics it is necessary to realize clearly, but at the same time to avoid, the verbal confusion which has arisen from the marked similarity between the way emotions feel and the way music sounds. Emotions are internal experiences. As felt, they run their course and are located within the body of the person who has them. The human body is the sounding board for the reverberations of all the complicated patterns of emotion, so that if a person could describe adequately how it feels, for example, to be agitated, he would probably refer to general bodily restlessness, trembling, rapid shooting sensations in various muscles, possibly draggings and pressures in the stomach, tingling of the hair, gritting of the teeth, etc. This whole internal bodily pattern or form is the material basis for the experience which is labelled agitation. But external forms composed of visual and auditory materials also assume shapes and patterns which closely resemble internal bodily disturbances. Music may *sound* agitated. The tempo is more rapid, the dynamics louder and harsher, the tonal design is thicker, the interval-leaps are wider and more dissonant, etc. Such a tonal pattern is fittingly described as one of agitation, but music of this kind, or of any other kind, is not itself an emotion, nor need it give rise in the listener to any real emotion. *Music sounds the way an emotion feels.*

This interpretation of the relation of emotion to music avoids the difficulties of older solutions which aestheticians have offered, and is also closer to the facts of musical experience. Music does not embody or contain emotion. This is psychologically impossible. Nor need it give rise to real emotion in the listener. Yet more than any other art, music is the language of emotion, the objective medium for the expression of the life of the spirit. Great composers weave kaleidoscopic patterns of sound which follow the contours of emotional patterns as they originate in the subjective experience of the composers' own lives. Only from this point of view does it make psychological sense to say that tonal design is the objectification of the subjective, that music is the language of emotion.[1]

Music sounds the way emotions feel. With this statement we are very close to our goal. Dr. Pratt, from whom the two

[1] Carroll C. Pratt, "The Relation of Emotion to Musical Value." *Volume of Proceedings*, 1938, Music Teachers National Association.

previous paragraphs are quoted, indicates that even though music sounds the way emotions feel it does not necessarily follow that it will give rise to real emotion in the listener. This is perfectly true, but every intelligent and sensitive listener will agree with Dr. Pratt's hesitant "yet" when he goes on to say that "more than any other art, music is the language of emotion." The "yet" implies that much music does give rise to real emotion in the listener. Certainly when the listener fails to be moved by moving music, he is missing the composer's message. We *are* moved by music.

The title of this chapter is "How Music Talks." So far in our attempt to explain the "how" we have arrived at two conclusions:

Music sounds the way emotions feel.
The listener can be moved by music.

The final answer to our "how" depends upon bringing these two conclusions together. "Music sounds the way emotions feel" is a statement that places music outside the listener, but when he is moved by music he is moved within himself. How is the moving contour of the music communicated to the listener's interior being? Psychologists have not answered that question, nor has anyone else, but we know that a kind of induction must take place. We know that when we are completely aware of and sensitive to a piece of music we go along with the music.

Here, then, is the substance of how music talks:

Emotion is motion.
Music is motion.
Music sounds the way emotions feel.
The listener goes with the music.

Before we turn to a musical demonstration of how music talks it will be valuable to make a comparison. How, by comparison, does the method of a story teller who wishes to induce emotion differ from the method of a composer? Both refer to their own past experiences for the emotion they wish to represent and, by representing, present to their audience. Both take the next step—which must be to remember how the emotion felt. The composer stops there. He tries to reproduce the contour of how he felt (how he was moved) in his music. The story teller, however, must take one more step. He must remember the chain of incidents which caused his emotion. Then he must tell, in words, that chain of incidents or a similar chain. Both composer and author hope that the individuals in their audiences will go along with the music or the story: the listener with the contour of the music; the reader *through* the incidents of the story to a line of emotion. The story teller must tell his story because his medium is words. The composer need not tell a story, could not if he wished, because his medium is music.

The extra step—which the writer must make but which the composer cannot make—is the source of nearly all the misapprehension concerning the meaning of music. It is the difference between *describing* an experience or emotion— the extra step—and making the listener apprehend it directly.

Chapter 16

HEARING MUSIC TALK

THE problem of how to transmute the way emotions feel into the way music sounds has not been an easy one for composers. Just as an architect must know the structural strength of his materials before he can create a functional design, so must the composer understand the structural implications of his materials before he can explore their power as an emotional language. Some composers have been more successful, and more often successful, than others. In music, too, as in other languages, certain styles have come to have an archaic sound. It is as difficult for the average listener to feel the living pulse in music that to him sounds archaic as for the ordinary reader to feel the human qualities of Chaucer. When we call a composer great, it is because enough listeners, over a long enough period of time, have felt that his music has the power of speaking to them. He has, within the limitations of the style of his own time, spoken, in musical sounds, in a *moving* way—with an authentic voice.

A demonstration of music which will move the listener might begin at almost any point in the history of music. To make the demonstration not too difficult for the listener several things have been taken into account. First, a point must have been reached where composers no longer take a childlike pleasure in the tricks that they can do with music;

the technic of musical construction, in other words, must have ceased to be an end in itself. Second, the style must have vitality for modern listeners. Finally, a point must have been reached where composers are learning, with increasing penetration, that form, even musical form, is the *form of experience*—not that form and content are separate entities, but that content cannot exist until it has taken form.

In describing how a knowledge of the conventional forms can give guidance in listening, Mozart's music has been ideal for purposes of illustration. Lest the reader suspect that Mozart spoke only the language of formal perfection, let us now turn to Mozart's music for a demonstration of how music talks. It is quite true that Mozart lived in a period when formality was a kind of substitute for spontaneous speech—a time when it would have been impolite to give public utterance to the deepest emotions. Occasionally Mozart was, in that eighteenth-century sense, impolite. Two movements of the Quintet in G minor (K.V. 516) will show us the *man* under the powdered wig.

Play the first movement until its thematic structure is familiar. The themes themselves are easy to find. It is clearly in the sonata form.

First theme:

Second theme:

Closing episode (motto):

The listener recognizes the minor quality of the harmony, the almost monotonous feeling of the repeated notes in the accompanying parts, and the somberness of the melodic lines. Most listeners would be willing to agree with one of Mozart's biographers, who said of this quintet that it is a "deeply-felt work . . . yielding, forcibly, a picture of bitter resignation." Is it possible to analyze the contour of this music so that the listener can feel with conviction that its moving qualities are inherent in the music? Let us try.

The contour of the first theme gives the first hint. It begins with an upward thrust, but moves over the depressed minor third:

The upward thrust carries to the first note of the answering fragment, but from that high point the melodic line sags— loses energy—to the end of the phrase. The accompaniment also marks the downward motion:

Notice, in the middle of the second measure of this long descending passage, the unsuccessful effort of the melody to break away from the downward pull. The contour of the line so far has been a short, almost energetic rise, followed by a long descent:

The long descent ends, moreover, on an active harmony, which pushes the music forward to the next phrase. Here

the melodic group which corresponds to the rise at the beginning has the opposite motion, as if the loss of energy had
had its effect:

This is answered by a rising line in which every small group
of notes ends by falling away from its high point:

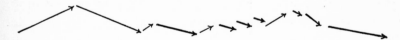

The music is right back where it started; but hear what the
'cello does immediately. It moves to a much lower point:

Then, with the somber tone-quality of the 'cello and two
violas and the music moving an octave lower, the whole
pattern is repeated:

It should be noted that the upward thrusts of the second
half of the viola's melody are followed by a more decided
falling off. The loss of energy is accentuated:

At the point where all five instruments play together for
the first time, which marks the bridge between first and

second themes, the music has reached a climax by picking itself up by its bootstraps. It has called forth a comparatively tremendous display of energy. Notice how it falls away from that climax to a point where the used-up energy has depressed and slowed down the whole fabric. Perhaps the most poignant effect comes when the violins appear unable to reach high enough to maintain the normal tones of the key:

The bridge ends with repetitions of the falling figure of the first theme:

This brings the listener to the second theme. If he has been listening carefully he makes an amazing discovery. The music has not developed energy enough to move to a new key. It hasn't arrived anywhere! The ineffectual, self-consuming vigor of the bridge passage has resulted only in a fall back into the minor key in which the music began. As the second theme unfolds, the reason for this becomes clear. The monotony of the accompaniment continues, but, more important, the second theme gives a new and more poignant emphasis to the drooping quality of the music, which it could not do if it had followed the rule that calls for the second theme to be in the major:

Notice that the three high points in this melodic line are on the flatted sounds of the key—the sounds from which the normal progression is downward.

First and second theme sound different—they grow out of different motives—but they are talking about the same emotional contour:

As the music continues, notice how this contour determines everything the music does. The bridge to the closing episode is introduced by first violin and violoncello with this almost stumbling version:

The high passage is an elongation of the upward-thrusting aspect of the contour, but the motto of the closing episode insists on the downward aspect:

The exposition ends with an emphasis on the upward motion, another attempt to force the music to accumulate energy:

But the beginning of the development gives the answer:

The conflict between the two opposing aspects of the contour continues through the development, which finally falls back into the recapitulation. The recapitulation retraces the contours that by now have become inevitable. The coda adds new poignancy to the drooping quality as it summarizes the idea which has dictated, throughout the movement, the contour of the music. Notice the effect of the descending chromatic scales in the first violin against the second theme in other parts of the fabric, while a reiterated organ point in the second viola emphasizes to the end the monotonous quality of the forward motion.

The two final chords may perhaps sound out of character. They must be understood as a kind of punctuation mark— a bow that Mozart made toward convention, after having composed an unconventional piece of music. The artificial quality of such an ending adds emphasis to what has preceded it.

Turn now to the fourth movement of the same Mozart quintet. It is slow and rather short and serves as an introduction to the final movement. It has no ending of its own, but leads directly to the forced liveliness of music which, although it is in a major key and is dancelike in character, has this main subject:

Because its function is partly that of introducing the final movement, this slow movement says what it has to say with absolute directness. When its message has been uttered, it goes about the business of preparing for what is to come next.

The listener should play this movement several times to discover how well he can follow its contour. He must notice a good many things: Its pace is slow, and it is carried forward by the constantly reiterated eighth notes of the inner voices. Notice how one after another of these middle parts tries to break away from the monotonous repetition by moving downward and upward, but finally subsides on its straight-line forward motion. The second violin part at the beginning is characteristic:

Under this the violoncello treads more slowly, in plucked notes, across the tones of the tonic chord:

The first violin begins its melodic line, which has something of the quality of impromptu speech, with a phrase that frankly loses energy in its downward movement. The violin phrase is immediately echoed an octave lower by the violoncello:

The violin answers with a characteristic contour:

This much of the music has the function of setting the emotional stage. The inner voices try to squirm out of their monotony. The violoncello begins with a rising thrust, only to fall back, after the frank depression of the first violin's phrase, to an echo of that part. Then the first violin's second utterance makes a vigorous upward thrust, only to fail, after a second attempt, to maintain its highest point. The upward motion of the first violin has, however, swung the music to the activity of the dominant harmony, which makes possible a repetition of the whole statement on a higher level:

The upward shift of one tone is important. It indicates what the composer has in mind. He is making music that is attempting to lift itself, in the face of the fact that that lifting must be done in spite of all its normal tendencies. It is trying to achieve an elevation, an elation, which requires that it overcome its stronger, more insistent depression. The continuation of the melodic line displays the contour of the process:

At the high note the melodic line has struggled to its highest point. The effort it makes to stay there is superlative. The underlying parts add as much strength as possible to the effort. Notice the effect of their movement and the increasing volume of the sound. After five strenuous attempts to maintain the high point as a goal, with a further falling back after each attempt, the climax of the whole effort is a sudden quiet and failure to regain the high point:

After the failure to reach the high point the line stumbles down as though its energy were dissipated. From that failure to achieve a climax the music makes one last try, as an echo of what has gone before:

At that point the music stops "talking" to move rather aimlessly, as far as its emotional contour is concerned, to the next movement.

It is rather difficult to write calmly of this movement. It is impossible for the listener who has discovered what to hear to listen calmly. The final failure of the melodic line to reach what it has spent so much effort to attain and to maintain is a kind of musical futility which must parallel the emotion the composer wished to communicate. It is impossible to believe that such music was accidental. It is impossible not to be moved by it. It is impossible to understand it without understanding the little man under the wig—Mozart.

Play it again!

RECORDING

Mozart   String Quintet in G minor (K.V. 516)   Victor M-190

Chapter 17

BEETHOVEN LEARNS TO TALK

LUDWIG VAN BEETHOVEN was prevented from taking lessons from Mozart by a series of misfortunes which culminated in Mozart's death. The younger man felt an intense curiosity about what lay beyond the gate which Mozart had opened in music like the Quintet in G minor. It was a new world; he had to explore it for himself.

Beethoven wrote at the top of the first page of his "Missa Solemnis" ("Solemn Mass"): "Von Herzen—Möge es zu Herzen gehen." It is difficult for anyone to affirm what the preceding three chapters have attempted to place before the listener with any greater emphasis than that: *"This comes from the heart—may it go to the heart."*

How did Beethoven know that he had composed music from the heart? One of the reasons he knew was that he had taught himself how to do it. Would it be possible for us, as listeners, to confirm our understanding of how music talks by watching Beethoven teach himself how to make music talk? A visit to Beethoven's workshop should be illuminating. It must not be inferred, however, from the title of this chapter that he began his efforts to learn to talk only with the music we are about to discuss.

Beethoven's first symphony was composed during the years 1799 and 1800 and was first performed at Vienna in April,

1800. In this work Beethoven opened the door not only to his own series of symphonies but to the century in which all composers were to be preoccupied with the problem of the expressive power of music.

It is not strange that the generation which emphasized the dignity and limitless perfectibility of the individual human being should have produced composers who had confidence in the importance of what they, as individuals, had to say. It is not strange that a generation which produced the "Liberty, Equality, Fraternity" of the French Revolution and such documents as the American Declaration of Independence should also have produced a Beethoven. It would be a perverse reckoning of the importance of individuals to the now rather wistful hopes of mankind which could omit Beethoven's name from any list of the men who have given urgent form to a statement of those hopes. Few voices have said with greater emphasis that "all mankind are brothers plighted." [1] This great composer stood at the threshold of a new world, a world to which his music must speak. He had to learn to make it speak. No small part of Beethoven's greatness is due to his tenacity of purpose. He did learn.

The first symphony, Symphony No. 1 in C major, Op. 21, can show us how he learned.

As the listener attempts to penetrate the meaning of an extended musical work it is more important than ever to hear the music completely. To this end the ability to follow the materials and forms of music must continue to be cultivated. The listener who is lost in the music cannot hope to discover its meaning. The starting point for all listening must be the pattern of the music. To that end, the listener must make himself a mental map of the music. Such maps

[1] Beethoven's Ninth Symphony.

for Beethoven's first symphony follow. The important theme is given in ordinary notation before the diagram in each case.

FIRST MOVEMENT

First theme

Second theme

Closing episode

Beethoven, Symphony No. 1, First Movement — Sonata Form

Exposition

Slow Introduction	First Theme	—	Bridge passage — Second Theme — Bridge passage — Closing episode

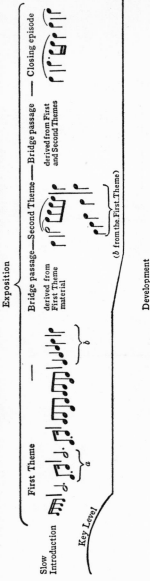

First Theme

Bridge passage
derived from
First Theme
material

Second Theme

Bridge passage
derived from First
and Second Themes

Closing episode

a

b

(*b* from the First Theme)

Key Level

Development

Motives of First and Second Theme Material

Recapitulation

First Theme	—	Bridge passage	—	Second Theme	—	Bridge passage	—	Closing episode	—	Coda

First Theme
Full orchestra, loud,
shorter than in the
exposition

Bridge passage
Based this time on
different material
than in the exposition:

Second Theme
Somewhat different
orchestration. Normal
Key for recapitulation.

Bridge passage
Similar to
exposition.

Closing episode
Similar to
exposition.

Coda
Uses material
of First Theme

 of First Theme

SECOND MOVEMENT

First theme

Second theme

Closing episode

Beethoven, Symphony No. 1, Second (Slow) Movement — Sonata Form

Exposition

First Theme — Bridge passage — Second Theme — Bridge passage — Closing episode

Enters in imitation

(violins)

(kettle drum)

Development

First and Second Theme material plus kettle-drum rhythm from closing episode

Recapitulation

First Theme — Bridge passage — Second Theme — Bridge passage — Closing episode — Coda

First Theme: Adds counter-melody, first in violoncello:

Bridge passage: Same material as in the exposition

Second Theme: Slightly different orchestration than in the exposition. Normal key for the recapitulation.

Bridge passage: Similar to exposition

Closing episode: Similar to exposition

Coda: Extended, based on First Theme and kettle-drum rhythm of the closing episode

THIRD MOVEMENT

Minuet *a*:

Minuet *b*:

Minuet *c* (Trio)

etc.

Minuet *d* (Trio)

Beethoven, Symphony No. 1, Third Movement — Minuet Form

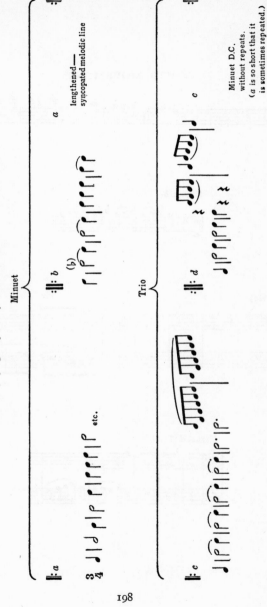

FOURTH MOVEMENT

First theme

Second theme

Closing episode

199

Beethoven, Sympony No. 1, Fourth Movement—Sonata Form

Exposition

Short
Introduction

First Theme —

Bridge passage —

and

Second Theme —

not in normal
key, but in the
dominant of the
dominant.

etc.

Bridge passage — Closing episode

(First Theme)

(repeat is often made)

Development

Based on material of the First Theme

Recapitulation

First Theme

shorter than in
the exposition

Bridge passage

first motive of
exposition bridge
(see above) is
extended; second
is omitted.

Second Theme

longer than in
the exposition.
normal key for
the recapitulation.

Bridge passage

same as in the
exposition ex-
cept for key.

Closing episode

similar to
exposition.
ending leads
to the coda.

Coda

Extended,
material from
development,
First Theme,
first Bridge
passage.

When we have acquainted ourselves well with this symphony, we are ready to analyze the music from the standpoint of Beethoven's care to give it an emotional contour. We need not expect a profound emotional experience, but we will find that, beyond question, Beethoven was thinking of a unified expression for the whole symphony, to which each of the movements should contribute its part. He was transmuting the conventional forms which he inherited into a new form for which we have no name because it cannot be conventionalized. The whole symphony develops and displays an emotional contour. Here, as with the Mozart music, the thematic material gives the clue.

FIRST MOVEMENT

The first theme emphasizes, with imperative strength, the level of the key. It does this by making upward thrusts to that level, and the thrusts establish what has been mentioned previously as the strongest musical relationship—that of dominant-tonic. After an upward thrust between two long notes, the music gathers too much energy to wait for long notes, and doubles the rate of its upward motion. This accumulation of energy pushes the keynote up an octave over a series of notes, the last three of which are again an echo of the upward motive:

This first theme is not the beginning of the symphony. The introduction cannot be understood, however, except in the light of the first theme's extraordinary insistence on the tonic. If the first theme were the first music the listener hears, its long tonic harmony would be felt only as a starting point. Placing it so that it becomes a consummation of a previous process makes its long tonic seem important and fresh. The introduction, which begins on a dissonant chord in a foreign key—and how that horrified some of Beethoven's contemporaries!—leads to and emphasizes the strength and vitality of the first theme. The sudden change of pace from slow to fast is also not without effect.

The first theme actually begins with a four-note falling figure, which in this case has no feeling of depression, but rather one of consummation. The suspended feeling of a long dominant is satisfied:

The first theme, then, borrows part of its strength from the introduction, which, in turn, has its justification and purpose in the importance it gives to the first theme.

After the first statement of this theme the music does what more experience will lead the listener to expect of Beethoven's themes—it transplants itself one step upward. Beethoven's themes do this because so many of them contain the upward thrusting strength which makes such a leap possible.

Here, then, in a short introduction and two statements of a theme, the listener must recognize a tremendous vital energy. Everything that happens to the first theme adds to that energy. The following is one sample:

The hurrying upward tension breaks the motive pattern.

The second theme is a distinct contrast. Its mood is quiet, its quality lyrical, and part of its motion is downward. The loss of energy is not real; too many of the qualities of the first theme are present. The second theme begins with the same rise from dominant to tonic—in the new key—that characterized the first theme, and the whole downward motion is counteracted by the appearance of the last five notes of the first theme in the accompaniment:

Beethoven gives short shrift to even the very slight pensive quality which he leaves to the second theme. After an almost boisterous passage which serves as a bridge, but not to a new theme, he shows the true quality of the second theme. It sinks, in the violoncello, down through the music to the bottom, only to turn around and come back, with a burst of energy, to the first theme motive, which is the bridge to the closing episode. Compare this passage with the drooping music we heard from Mozart.

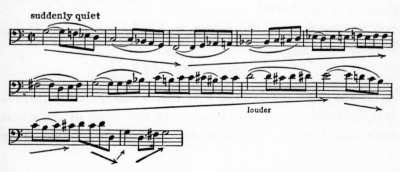

Even the apparent drop at the very end is counteracted by
the first violin and by the fact that, like the initial drop into
the first violin, it is the consummation of a long harmonic
circle. Experience of Beethoven's style will show that such
a long harmonic circle, ending in a burst of accumulated
energy, is an important characteristic.

The bridge to the closing episode continues the accumulation by insisting on the two strong motives of the first theme,
the first one now piled up in an imitation:

The second motive:

The closing episode hammers insistently on the upward
motion:

The general purpose of this movement should now be
clear. The development adds to the intensification. Near its
end it even inverts the figure with which the first theme
began:

After the development the first theme cannot enter quietly
as it did originally. It enters with the full force of the whole
orchestra. Then, for a bridge to the second theme, Beethoven

uses the falling first five notes of the first theme against a long rising harmonic progression. It is a final denial of the early weak element of the first theme, and that was weak only to the extent of moving downward.

The coda begins quietly with an attempt, in the descending lines of the woodwinds, to depress the first theme material. That attempt, in failing, adds one more emphasis to the vitality of the music. The ending is a burst of energy so great that it is a tremendous effort to get the movement stopped. Here is music to which the brakes have to be applied gradually to prevent the listener's going through the windshield.

The first movement has been, for the listener, a remarkable accumulation of energy and vitality, marked by themes which all have the elation of upward motion. The surge of strength sounds the way Beethoven wanted the listener to feel. Its perception is far more important for the understanding of Beethoven than any mere ability to notice that Beethoven used a conventional form. Beethoven is learning to be Beethoven: later he will acquire still more subtlety and grandeur of purpose.

SECOND MOVEMENT

The second movement, in a quieter mood, has exactly the same fundamental subject as the first. The important motive of the first theme is the two rising notes:

The imitative entrances of the first theme emphasize its strength.

The bridge to the second theme continues the accumulation of energy. The second theme emphasizes even more strongly than the first the rising pairs of notes:

The bridge to the closing episode begins with a rising figure whose crisp rhythm is a new sign of vigor:

It leads to the closing episode with a strong emphasis on the ascending pairs:

The closing episode introduces a new variety of energy in the rapid violin part over a long organ point in the kettledrums, violoncellos, and basses:

At the very end of the exposition the music says, "Now, if you haven't discovered what this is all about, listen":

The development is noteworthy for the manner in which it sticks to the subject. At no time is the listener permitted to be more than a short moment away from the rising contour, which may be derived from either first or second themes. To this is added the insistent rhythm of the kettledrum part from the closing episode:

One aspect of this development is especially interesting from the standpoint of the contour. At the fourth measure after the kettledrum takes its rhythmic figure from the strings, the music starts a harmonic curve that will lead eventually to the key of the recapitulation. The chords descend against the organ point of the tympani, but they descend in rising pairs:

The recapitulation again demonstrates how the subject matter has been accumulating energy. The first theme now brings with it a rapidly moving countersubject, which marches up and down across the fabric of the music:

The coda brings another example of the ability of this music to increase in vitality. It begins with a reminder of the first theme. The violins soon take up a reiteration of a single tone, in sixteenth notes, which insists on being heard after it has started very quietly. The lift of its upward motion is tremendous:

After this high point the music settles back to the strength of the kettledrum rhythm, heard in the strings, and ends with a final statement of the basic contour. As the music comes to an end the rhythmic movement becomes a scale, first downward and then both downward and upward:

Here, again, Beethoven has discussed, in terms of the contour of the music, exactly the same emotions of strength and vitality that furnished the subject for the first movement. The mood of the second movement is quieter, less hurried, but the fundamental purpose is the same. These two movements belong to the same symphony not because they were accidentally composed about the same time but because they are parts of the same idea.

THIRD MOVEMENT

Beethoven calls this movement a minuet, but he marks its speed as *allegro molto e vivace*—very fast and vivacious. In spirit it is about as far away from the traditional minuet as it could be; it anticipates the type of music for which Beethoven was later to use the word "scherzo."

Here the upward thrust from one tone to a higher piles up into a scale:

The *b* part of the minuet proper uses the same contour with only slightly less exuberance:

After a forcible descent this becomes a scale fragment:

To lead back to *a,* over a gradually ascending line in the violins, the low strings and the oboe and bassoon answer back and forth:

The return of *a* is extended in a passage in which the forward motion tips over into a long syncopation:

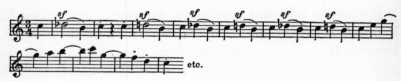

In the trio the chief rhythm of the minuet proper is carried forward, decorated by scale passages whose speed is sufficient indication of their enormous vivacity:

The *b* section of the trio breaks this material up into smaller groups and again uses the device of syncopation. The music is moving forward so energetically that it cannot wait for the normal three-beat pattern:

1 2 3 | 1 **2** 3 | 1 2**3** | **1** 2 3 | 1

To reproduce the effect of this syncopation, read aloud the numbers in the bottom line, emphasizing those printed in large type.

Beethoven's plan for this symphony is three-quarters finished. He is talking about the emotional contours that result
from accumulation of energy. The moods of strength of the
first two movements have given way in this third movement
to a vivacious display of good spirits. Would it be beyond
the realm of possibility for Beethoven next to play a practical joke on his listeners? Could good healthy horseplay be
a subject for music, and if so, could it come as a logical development from the first three movements of this symphony?

FOURTH MOVEMENT

The final movement begins with a slow introduction:

It builds up, with the utmost solemnity, a scale on the dominant: the long-held first note, then three-, four-, five-, six-,
and seven-note scale groups. Notice the mock hesitancy with
which the top note of the six-note group is touched, and the
delicacy of the last group. This is Beethoven's way of fore-
warning the listener that, first and second themes notwith-
standing, this movement is going to be about scales.

As we follow it we will hear scales pell-mell from all directions, plain scales, hidden scales, all sorts of scales. The
energy of the preceding movements has burgeoned in a
wilderness of scales.

After the lesson in scale anatomy of the introduction the
first theme begins—*allegro molto e vivace,* like the third
movement—with a scale:

The theme itself is but a decoration of *do-re-mi*. Immediately the violins sing an elaborated downward scale, with rising scales below:

This is followed by:

and then:

which is answered in the bass by:

Then comes the second theme, which is a jolly elaboration of a scale. It should be noticed that, appropriately among all these scales, the second theme emphasizes the tone D, one scale-step higher than the key of the first theme:

After this phrase is repeated, the theme, which now has a running start, becomes much more frankly an elaborated scale:

The exposition closes with the same scales, rhythmically, that the first theme began with:

But the fun has just begun. Hear for yourself how scales govern the development and how they are used in the coda. Notice at the end how long it takes to get this exuberance stopped.

This final movement of Beethoven's First Symphony has been called banal—unworthy of its composer. It is difficult to describe a piece of music with one word, but certainly the use of such a word indicates a complete failure to understand this movement as the natural outcome for Beethoven, at the age of twenty-nine, of the tremendous accumulation of energy in the former movements.

Beethoven was learning. In his hands the whole symphony has a plan. That plan controls the contours of the music, and, by controlling them, makes every aspect of it—tone-color, rhythm, melodic line, harmony, form—contribute to the fundamental idea. In his hands and by his example, music in the nineteenth century was to enter a new world.

RECORDINGS

Beethoven	First Symphony in C major, Op. 21	Victor M-73
		Victor M-409
		Victor M-507
		Columbia M-321

Part Three

INDEPENDENT LISTENING

Chapter 18

THE VISTA

THE purpose of this book so far has been to help the listener perceive how composers use musical sounds as an intelligible language—perceive how composers, using the language of music, create the literature of music. By tracing the composer's use of musical sounds, the listener learns how to listen and moves toward an independent ability to understand music. He now has the means for that independence. Of course there are other forms than those we have discussed, other styles, other composers. But other forms and styles and composers may be approached in the same way that we have learned to listen.

The literature of music is vast. No listener, no musician, can know more than a very small segment of it. But as a listener approaches that literature some suggestions about where to turn his attention should be valuable. The rest of this book will attempt to furnish such hints.

Music is essentially a method of human communication through the medium of ordered sounds. As we listen to music that is strange or new to us it is well to remember that fact. Modes of thought and expression change from one period to another, but the need to communicate the ideas for which music is the best medium is permanent. Music which at first repels the listener, which seems by its style to defy comprehension, will often reveal an inward order of its own to the listener who bears in mind that it, too, is human. Contact with unfamiliar music, taking in new styles, detecting the principles of contrast and repetition in novel fabrics and forms, can be an adventure of great delight.

THE SYMPHONY

The symphony, for the ordinary listener, begins with Haydn and Mozart. Symphonies were composed before Haydn, and hundreds were written by other composers during his lifetime, but they are seldom heard today. Haydn and Mozart are often mentioned in the same breath because they were both giants, because they were contemporaries, and because they learned from each other. Their dates will show the interesting relationship in the span of their lives:

Haydn 1732-1809
Mozart 1756-1791

Haydn was already famous as a composer while Mozart was a child prodigy. When Mozart had composed his greatest works and died at thirty-five, Haydn still had eighteen fruitful years before him.

The "must" symphonies of Mozart are the last two: No. 40, the Symphony in G minor, which we have already listened to carefully, and No. 41, the Symphony in C major, the "Jupiter." At least a dozen others will more than repay the effort of making their acquaintance.

The Haydn symphonies that are best known to modern audiences are those that were written for London during visits there in 1790-92 and 1794-95. Of these the two known as the "Clock," No. 4 in D major, and the "Surprise," No. 6

in G major, are the most popular. These so-called London symphonies were composed after the death of Mozart; they show Haydn at the height of his powers. They are altogether delightful, and no music lover can afford not to know them.

The great successor to Haydn and Mozart was Beethoven. In his hands the symphony came of age. Each of Beethoven's symphonies is a monumental human document in its own special way. We have already listened to the First. A good order in which to continue with them is: Third, Fifth, Second, Fourth, Eighth, Sixth, Seventh, Ninth; but there is no compulsion or absolute necessity about this. No new listener should expect to understand them immediately. Some of the elements of their greatness are inner relationships which become apparent to the listener often after the music has stopped sounding—sometimes long after. It is a mistake to read too much about them; they have been discussed from the special viewpoints of several generations, which do not always make sense for us of the twentieth century. The listener should let Beethoven, through his music, do most of the talking.

With Beethoven, it should be noticed, the symphony became more difficult to compose. Haydn composed in the neighborhood of one hundred and twenty-five symphonies, Mozart forty-one, Beethoven only nine. As we move on into the nineteenth century even nine will seem a large output for one man.

Franz Schubert lived in Vienna at the same time as Beethoven and died in the year after him (1828), but he was too shy to make acquaintance with the older man except through his music. He left at least two symphonies without which we would be much poorer. The "Unfinished," No. 8 in B minor, is his most famous. It is greater than any of the pieces that have been mined from it could possibly indicate. Notice how Schubert uses the melody with which he begins the first movement as a frame around the themes of the conventional sonata form. Here is the theme:

This introduces the movement, furnishes the material by which the music moves to the development, and gives the basis of most of the development; then it returns again in the coda. But it is not first or second theme or closing episode.

Schubert's Symphony No. 7 in C major is a gigantic work of haunting beauty. At the hands of a great conductor and orchestra, its length—it lasts almost an hour—is a convincing proof of the genius of its composer.

Only two symphonies that are heard with any frequency were composed in France during the whole of the nineteenth century. The first of these is the "Symphonie Fantastique" by Hector Berlioz, which illustrates many of the forces by which the composers of the nineteenth century were inspired. The "Fantastic" Symphony is an important landmark because of the way Berlioz used a verbal explanation to tell the listener what he was attempting to make the music say. The verbal explanation is called a program, from which we get the expression "program music."

Berlioz' verbal program runs like this:

A young musician of morbid sensibility and ardent imagination poisons himself with opium in a fit of amorous despair. The narcotic dose, too weak to result in death, plunges him into a heavy sleep accompanied by the strangest visions, during which his sensations, sentiments, and recollections are transformed in his sick brain into musical thoughts and images. The beloved woman herself has become for him a melody like a fixed idea which he finds and hears everywhere.

The melody "like a fixed idea" begins like this:

The titles of the movements identify the "strangest visions." The listener must hear what the music does, must follow not only the appearances of the "fixed idea" but the different forms it takes and the effect its appearances have on the music which follows them, and ought not imagine too much story. With the roll of the kettledrums and the melody played by the English horn and oboe in the third movement, and also with the waltz rhythm in the ball scene and the "Dies Irae" [1] melody in the last movement, Berlioz asks the listener to make direct (and truthful) associations with his own experience. The "Symphonie Fantastique" is a tremendously interesting work.

The symphonies of Mendelssohn, especially the two known as the "Scotch" and "Italian," appear with some frequency on concert programs. Mendelssohn's style is refreshingly clear. Nineteenth century interest in musical qualities apparently peculiar to individual countries is reflected in these symphonies, which also display Mendelssohn's brilliant handling of the orchestra. Notice particularly the salterello, the fast Italian dance with which the "Italian" Symphony ends.

Schumann composed four symphonies, heard less often than they deserve, because they are full of difficulties for the conductor. Schumann's great work for piano and orchestra, the Piano Concerto in A minor, written for his wife, is often played and has been recorded by several pianists. It contains

[1] Berlioz uses (and caricatures) the ancient plain-song melody to the "Wrath of God" text of the requiem mass.

some of the most truly inspired music of the nineteenth century. The first movement sings its way into the listener's mind with gentle strength, and the second movement, with its altogether charming musical dialogue, summons him, over a reminiscence of the first movement, to the great vitality of the last.

The four symphonies of Johannes Brahms are a contribution to symphonic literature which for most listeners establishes his title to a place in the three B's: Bach, Beethoven, Brahms. Each movement of each symphony is a masterpiece, and each symphony speaks with moving warmth and richness. But Brahms's music is not intended to be light entertainment; it holds the listener off, and its fabric is not easily penetrated.

The symphonies of Tchaikovsky have won a special place in the affections of most music lovers. The last three of his six have beaten down the opposition which met them at first. Even though critics condemned them, listeners soon found that these symphonies were profoundly moving musical experiences. They are the honest, sincere expression of a man of great genius who was tortured by his pathological inability to adjust himself to life. They do not speak with a godlike quality of understanding and serenity, but discuss the hopeless depression of failure.

Since Brahms and Tchaikovsky, only a few composers have produced symphonies of the first rank. The one symphony of César Franck (D minor), the Belgian composer, is the other great symphony composed in France during the nineteenth century. It is worth studying for its chromatic style, its polyphonic fabric, and the way in which its themes accumulate from one movement to another. Once he understands its language, the listener will find that, from its first note to its very last, it speaks to him. Another notable symphony is the Fifth of the Bohemian, Anton Dvorak; he composed it while living in New York and Spillville, Iowa. He gave it the title "From the New World," and it is notable for the way in which it attempts to convey the spirit of America by using thematic material which is not borrowed from Negro and Indian music but suggested by it. The second movement, with its famous English horn melody, attracts many listeners. The kaleidoscopic use, in the last movement, of themes from previous movements gives an interesting example of a device in music which is similar to the flashback technic of the motion picture.

The symphonies of Mahler and Bruckner are heard less often than they deserve. They represent a mode of musical thought to which it is not always easy to be sympathetic. The symphonies of Sibelius, on the other hand, have attracted increasing interest. Most composers of great symphonies have framed the emotional contour of their music within a semblance of conventional forms and by the use of a melodic line growing out of well-defined motives. This is often Sibelius' procedure, but at times the listener must seek for the meaning in the contour alone, without assistance from conventional form and motive structure. This characteristic is not necessarily a fault; often it occasions effects of great interest.

Even a short discussion of symphonic literature would be incomplete without mention of the works of American composers. Symphonies by Howard Hanson and Roy Harris can be heard on phonograph records and are produced more and more often in concerts. The listener might ask himself, as he hears works by these men, if the aspects of the music which make for terseness and pace are not a portrayal, in terms of music, of emotional contours which have vitality and validity to twentieth century America.

THE SYMPHONIC POEM

We have seen that music is an ideal vehicle for the expression of emotion. We noted, moreover, that in producing an emotional reaction in the listener the composer takes one less step than a storyteller does. Because human beings often refer their emotions to external experiences which aroused them, just as the storyteller does, and because the emotions that come from music feel the same as those resulting from external experience, many listeners conceive of the meaning of music in terms of their own actual life. One of the implications of this process is that even when listeners perceive the same emotional contour—the same meaning—in a piece of music, they can hardly refer it to the same actual experiences and hence will apparently disagree as to its meaning. Most disagreements arise, however, from the fact that listeners really have not heard the same music; each has heard a different aspect of the same piece.

Composers have tried to get around this difficulty by indicating, when they could, the source of their ideas for their music. The help given by the composer is often a simple title like some that we have noticed in our brief discussion of symphonies. But as composers, especially during the nineteenth century, discovered more and more ways of establishing direct associations between music and other types of experience, as Berlioz did, this desire to indicate the source of ideas led to what has been called a new musical form, the symphonic or tone poem. The symphonic poem is not actually a new form in music. What is new about it is that its

use of the formal principle of repetition after contrast produces a series of connected musical episodes whose character
is dictated, at least in part, by its program. The program,
then, is the composer's verbal indication, more or less extended, of the source of his ideas.

The dramatic or operatic overture, when it attempts to
trace or prepare for the contour of the drama which it precedes, has much of the character of a symphonic poem.
Beethoven's overtures for his opera, *Fidelio* (*Leonora*), as
well as his overtures to plays like *Coriolan* and *Egmont*, are
of this type. Others are Weber's overtures to *Der Freischütz*,
Euryanthe, and *Oberon* and Wagner's overtures to *Rienzi*,
The Flying Dutchman, and *Tannhäuser* and the preludes to
Lohengrin, *Tristan and Isolda*, *Die Meistersinger*, and *Parsifal*.

These and other overtures and preludes, however, are not
of large enough dimensions to be symphonic poems as the
term has come to be used. For many composers, the symphonic poem has provided a substitute for, or successor to,
the symphony.

The listener's approach to a symphonic poem should be
primarily an attempt to understand the music. A search for
musical illustrations of incidents in the program too often
takes the place of really listening to the music. The whole
function of the program fails if the listener attends to the
story at the cost of the music.

There is an extensive and interesting literature of symphonic poems. Liszt's "Les Préludes" remains one of the most
interesting. If parts of it seem hackneyed, it is because his
descriptive episodes are so felicitous that they have been ap-
propriated wholesale for use on the sound track of moving-
picture films. Smetana, Sibelius, Rimsky-Korsakov, and Saint-

Saëns have had varying success with the symphonic poem. Rimsky-Korsakov's "Scheherazade" Suite is a set of four symphonic poems. Most important among composers of this type of music is Richard Strauss. His works are, for many listeners, the crown of symphonic program music. Most of them can be heard on phonograph records and are part of the permanent repertoire of all great symphony orchestras. They exhibit a high virtuosity in orchestral writing which grows out of Strauss's sensitivity to the resources of individual instruments and his feeling for great masses of sound.

The listener will do well to make acquaintance with Strauss through the symphonic poems "Don Juan" and "The Merry Pranks of Till Eulenspiegel." Hear them as a series of musical episodes which are connected by threads of thematic development and which appear in rondolike sequence. Then go on to the other, more massive works: "Death and Transfiguration," "Thus Spake Zarathustra," "Don Quixote"— a set of variations—and "A Hero's Life."

SONGS

Most songs literally speak for themselves. The first problem for the composer of a song has always been to combine music and text so that the text may receive the correct inflection and emphasis. As composers gained skill in conceiving and controlling the expressive contour of music, a new type of song came into existence, the art song or through-composed song. In the art song a further problem for the composer is that of reflecting in the music the emotional contour of the poem. When he is successful he makes music that is so welded with the text that neither music nor text can be thought of separately.

The literature of the art song furnishes a fascinating test-
ing place for the way in which music communicates. Try to
understand the text; then follow the motion of the music
as it reflects and amplifies the emotion of the poem. The
whole problem of understanding songs lies in perceiving and
feeling this relationship. Schubert's songs are an excellent
starting point; hundreds of them are worth knowing, and
many have been recorded. Among those that will not only
appeal to most listeners but will also furnish interesting illustrations of the way in which Schubert's music talks are "The
Erlking," "Atlas," "The Double," "The Guidepost," "The
Trout," "The Wanderer," "Death and the Maiden,"
"Gretchen at the Spinning Wheel," "My Lone Abode," and
"The Linden Tree."

Nearly every nineteenth century composer was interested
in the art song. Try to hear at least a few of the songs
of Schumann, Franz, Brahms, Wolf, Grieg, Tchaikovsky,
Strauss, Duparc, and Fauré.

OPERA

The greatest difficulty that opera presents to the American
listener, when he can hear it, is that of understanding the
words. There seems to be no help except in either learning
the drama ahead of time or letting a complete understanding
emerge very slowly from many hearings.

Opera combines music with drama. Hearing operatic
music is not different from hearing other music. The forms
of operatic songs or arias, insofar as they are musical forms,
grow out of the principles we have studied. The function of
music in the opera grows out of its ability to enhance the
emotional contour of the drama.

The musical methods of one great composer who confined himself almost altogether to composing for the stage call for some special description. Richard Wagner was one of the musical giants of the nineteenth century. His dissatisfaction with the traditions of opera and his belief that music drama had a vital social function to fulfill, together with the special qualities of his own genius, carried him into a field which he holds alone.

SOLO INSTRUMENTS AND CHAMBER MUSIC

A sketch of the domain covered by the literature of music would not be complete without some indication of the great riches that are to be found in music for solo instruments and for small groups of instruments.

The piano has attracted the sustained interest of almost every great composer. The listener must learn, however, to discern the difference between music composed for the purpose of technical display and music composed because its composer had something vital to say. The keyboard music of Bach and his predecessors, the volumes of piano sonatas of Haydn, Mozart, and Beethoven, and the piano music of Schubert, Schumann, Chopin, Liszt, and Brahms, will point the way into a magnificent literature.

Every instrument of the orchestra has attracted great composers to some degree. This is especially true of the violin and the violoncello. Because of their melodic nature, orchestral instruments usually play as a solo voice with piano accompaniment. The sonatas for violin and piano, extending from before Bach to the present day, contain a wealth of great music. Here, too, for the sake of a splendid literature which does not deserve to be forgotten, mention should be made of the violin music of Corelli, Nardini, Tartini, and Vivaldi. Sonatas for violoncello and piano cover, in a more limited way, about the same area of musical style.

The literature of concertos for solo instrument and orchestra contains much great music. Nearly every composer who has written for orchestra has written music of this type. Beginning with the concertos of Bach and his immediate predecessors, music for piano, violin, and other solo instruments with orchestra covers a wide range of styles.

Chamber music is for small groups of players and is to be performed in the intimate atmosphere of a small gathering. It is, moreover, music which has usually been composed not for a public audience, but for the composer's friends. For this reason a composer's chamber music may often be the truest expression of his genius. Traditional chamber music combinations are the trio for piano, violin, and violoncello; the quartet for two violins, viola, and violoncello, commonly called the string quartet; the quartet for piano, violin, viola, and violoncello; the quintet for two violins, two violas, and violoncello; and the quintet for piano and string quartet. Composers have occasionally written also for instrumental sextets, septets, and octets.

The music lover will find much that is unsurpassable in the chamber music of Haydn, Mozart, Beethoven, Schubert, Mendelssohn, Schumann, Brahms, and Franck, to say nothing of the composers of the twentieth century.

BACH

A book that tries to lead the listener to an appreciation of music would not be complete without some discussion of the problems involved in hearing the music of Bach. And that discussion belongs properly at the end of the book, chiefly because Bach's music requires experience.

Bach's music represents the apex of a long development in which music was composed and heard entirely as a polyphonic texture. Musicians have regarded that kind of music as a system of complex formulas. The consequent complexities disappear if the music is examined simply from the listener's standpoint.

The so-called polyphonic forms are, with one possible real exception, organized on the principle of repetition after contrast. That exception is based on a remarkably interesting device for using repetition and contrast at the same time—a device which we have already encountered in our study of the theme and variations. Polyphonic forms actually are textures. We know how textures must be heard. The texture of the fugue is characterized by the manner in which entrances of the thematic material appear one after another, in imitation. After these entrances have been made, the lines of the texture grow out of the motives of the subject matter. For contrast, the form depends on a change of key in the middle; it may be analyzed as *ABA*, depending not on change of subject matter but on change of key. The fugues of Bach's *Well-Tempered Clavichord* or his fugues for organ will provide magnificent examples.

The concerto texture is like that of the fugue except that it makes use of two sets of thematic material, comparable in some ways to the first and second themes of the sonata form. These subjects usually enter in imitation in several melodic lines. The first is called the tutti subject, because it is played by all the instruments; the second, the solo subject, because it is given to the solo instrument or group of instruments. Any or all of Bach's concertos for one or more pianos and orchestra or for one or more violins and orchestra, and also the "Brandenburg" Concertos, exhibit this texture. For the listener who wants to go back of these great riches to other music that does not deserve oblivion, the concertos of Corelli, Nardini, Vivaldi, Tartini, Handel, and a host of others will prove a treasure-trove. No music lover should miss Corelli's "Christmas" Concerto.

The so-called dance forms are all, with the exception already mentioned, of the *ABA* pattern. As in the other polyphonic forms, the contrast is in the key or mode, not in melodic material. Dance forms are usually short. Their texture in each case grows out of their rhythmic characteristics. Although musicians habitually call the dance forms polyphonic, their textures are often monophonic; because of that fact they are the ancestors of our ternary, rondo, minuet, and sonata forms. The names of the dance forms apply not to the forms as such but to the rhythmic figures and speeds which are characteristic of them. The listener will meet these forms as movements in partitas, suites, and sonatas (remember the different ways in which "sonata" has been used), under names like allemande, gavotte, pavane, sarabande, bourrée.

The polyphonic texture which uses repetition *with* contrast appears under a number of names such as chaconne, passacaglia, folia, or variation. Sometimes it is not given any characteristic name. One piece of subject matter is repeated over and over again, while around or above it is woven a texture of melodic lines, usually growing out of their own melodic motives. Such a texture may be very simple if the repetitions of the ground are literal and kept at the bottom of the music, or it may be complex if the repetitions change level and almost disappear through the process of variation.

A simple use of this texture occurs in the "Crucifixus" from Bach's Mass in B minor. Examples of its complex use are his famous Chaconne for solo violin, Passacaglia in C minor for organ, which has been transcribed for orchestra, and the "Goldberg" Variations.

Here, then, is a great literature, in which each listener will find something to interest him especially. His sympathies may lead him in directions which this book has not indicated. There is the vast treasure of religious music, extending from plain song through motet and anthem to oratorio. There is, too, the intensely interesting music of the twentieth century. Whatever he hears, his experience will show him the landmarks. Some of those landmarks will be great monuments, works of peculiar and enduring significance. It is not necessary to agree on a list of works to be thought of as monumental, but landmarks may be nearly the same for everyone. The last four chapters are intended to serve as a guide to some musical landmarks. After that the listener must use his independence.

RECORDINGS

Mozart	Symphony No. 41 in C major ("Jupiter")	Victor M-203
Haydn	Symphony No. 4 in D major ("Clock")	Victor M-57
	Symphony No. 6 in G major ("Surprise")	Victor M-55
Beethoven	Second Symphony in D major, Op. 36	Victor M-131 Columbia M-302, M-377
	Third Symphony ("Eroica") in E flat major, Op. 55	Victor M-263 Columbia M-285

	Fourth Symphony in B flat major, Op. 60	Victor M-676 Columbia M-197
	Fifth Symphony in C minor, Op. 67	Victor M-245 Columbia M-254
	Sixth Symphony ("Pastoral") in F major, Op. 68	Victor M-417 Columbia M-201
	Seventh Symphony in A major, Op. 92	Victor M-317 Columbia M-260
	Eighth Symphony in F major, Op. 93	Victor M-336 Columbia M-292
	Ninth Symphony ("Choral"), in D minor, Op. 125	Victor M-236 Columbia M-227
Schubert	Symphony No. 7 in C major	Victor M-268
	Symphony No. 8 ("Unfinished") in B minor	Victor M-319 Columbia M-330
Berlioz	Symphony No. 1 ("Fantastic") in C major, Op. 14a	Victor M-111 Columbia M-267
Mendelssohn	Symphony No. 3 ("Scotch") in A minor	Columbia M-126
	Symphony No. 4 ("Italian") in A major	Victor M-294 Columbia M-167
Schumann	Symphony No. 1 in B flat major, Op. 38	Victor M-86
	Symphony No. 3 ("Rhenish") in E flat major, Op. 97	Victor M-237
	Symphony No. 4 in D minor, Op. 120	Victor M-201 Columbia M-106
	Concerto in A minor for piano and orchestra, Op. 54	Victor M-39 Columbia M-196
Brahms	Symphony No. 2 in D major, Op. 73	Victor M-82 Columbia M-265

Brahms	Symphony No. 3 in F major, Op. 90	Victor M-341 Columbia M-353
	Symphony No. 4 in E minor, Op. 98	Victor M-185 Victor M-242 Columbia M-335
Tchaikovsky	Symphony No. 4 in F minor, Op. 36	Victor M-327 Columbia M-133
	Symphony No. 5 in E minor, Op. 64	Victor M-253 Columbia M-104
	Symphony No. 6 ("Pathétique") in B minor, Op. 74	Victor M-337 Columbia M-227
Franck	Symphony in D minor	Victor M-300 Columbia M-121
Dvorak	Symphony No. 5 ("From the New World") in E minor, Op. 95	Victor M-273 Columbia M-77
Mahler	Symphony No. 2 in C minor	Victor M-256
Bruckner	Symphony No. 4 ("Romantic") in E flat major	Victor M-331
	Symphony No. 7 in E major	Victor M-276
Sibelius	Symphony No. 1 in E minor, Op. 39	Victor M-290
	Symphony No. 2 in D major, Op. 43	Victor M-272
	Symphony No. 3 in C major, Op. 52 (together with Symphony No. 7)	Victor M-394
	Symphony No. 4 in A minor, Op. 63	Victor M-160
	Symphony No. 5 in E flat major, Op. 82	Victor M-333
	Symphony No. 6 in D minor, Op. 104	Victor M-344
	Symphony No. 7 in C major, Op. 105 (together with Symphony No. 3)	Victor M-394
Hanson	Symphony No. 2 ("Romantic"), Op. 30	Victor M-648

Harris	"Symphony: 1933"	Columbia M-191
	Symphony No. 3	Victor M-651
Beethoven	*Fidelio* Overture	Victor 11809
	"Leonora" No. 3 Overture	Victor M-359
	Coriolan Overture	Victor 11909
	Egmont Overture	Victor 7291
Weber	*Der Freischütz* Overture	Victor 12040
		Columbia 68986D
	Euryanthe Overture	Victor 12037
		Columbia 68069D
	Oberon Overture	Victor 12043
		Columbia 69410D
Wagner	*Rienzi* Overture	Victor 6624, 6625
	Flying Dutchman Overture	Victor 9275
	Tannhäuser Overture	Victor 9059, 9060
		Columbia Set X-123
	Lohengrin, Prelude to Act I	Victor 6791
	Tristan and Isolda, Prelude to Act I	Victor 6585
	Die Meistersinger, Prelude to Act I	Victor 6858, 6859
Smetana	"Moldau"	Victor 11434, 11435
Sibelius	"Night Ride and Sunrise"; "The Oceanides"	Victor M-333
Rimsky-Korsakov	"Scheherazade" Suite	Victor M-269
Saint-Saëns	"Danse Macabre"	Victor 14162
	"Phaëton"	Victor 11431
Strauss	"The Merry Pranks of Till Eulenspiegel"	Columbia 67478D, 67479D
	"Death and Transfiguration"	Victor M-217
	"Thus Spake Zarathustra"	Victor M-257
	"Don Quixote"	Victor M-144
	"A Hero's Life"	Victor M-44
Schubert	"The Erlking"	Columbia 67431D
		Brunswick 90432
		H.M.V. ER 294
	"Atlas"	Columbia 67434D
	"The Double"	Columbia 67435D
	"The Guidepost"	Columbia 67432D
	"The Trout"	Columbia 67434D
	"The Wanderer"	Columbia 67431D
	"Death and the Maiden"	Columbia 67431D

Schubert	"Gretchen at the Spinning Wheel"	Columbia 7177M
	"My Lone Abode"	Columbia 67433D
	"The Linden Tree"	Columbia 67435D
Bach	*Well-Tempered Clavichord*, Vol. I, Nos. 1-17	Columbia M-120, M-147
	Toccata and Fugue in D minor (organ)	Columbia 68145D
	Concerto for two violins in D minor	Victor 7732, 7733
	Passacaglia in C minor (orchestral transcription)	Victor M-59
	"Brandenburg" Concerto No. 2	Victor M-59
	"Brandenburg" Concerto No. 6	Victor 11264, 11265
	Mass in B minor	Victor M-104
	Suite in D minor	Victor M-214
	French Suites, No. 5 and No. 6	Columbia M-200
	Sonata in C major (for violin alone)	Victor M-214
Corelli	"Christmas" Concerto	Columbia 68075D, 68076D
Vivaldi	Concerto in G minor	Victor 7585, 7586
Tartini	Sonata in G major	Columbia D1629, 1630
Handel	Six Concerti Grossi	Gramophone Shop Album No. 159

Chapter 19

TWO SYMPHONIC POEMS

LISZT: "LES PRELUDES"

What is our life but a series of preludes to that unknown song, the first solemn note of which is sounded by death? The enchanted dawn of every existence is heralded by Love, yet in whose destiny are not the first throbs of happiness interrupted by storms whose violent blasts dissipate his fond illusions, consuming his altar with fatal fire,—and where is to be found the cruelly bruised soul, that having become the sport of one of these tempests, does not seek oblivion in the sweet quiet of rural life? Nevertheless, man seldom resigns himself to the beneficent calm which at first chained him to Nature's bosom. No sooner does the trumpet sound the alarm than he runs to the post of danger, be the war what it may that summons him to its ranks. For there he will find again in the struggle complete self-realization and the full possession of his forces.

WITH this quotation from Lamartine's *Méditations, poétiques et religieuses,* as a guide and source of inspiration, Franz Liszt composed his third symphonic poem, "Les Préludes." The work was completed in 1850 and had its first performance at Weimar in 1854.

At the outset the listener must realize that there is no symphonic poem form comparable to the sonata form. Each symphonic poem will make its own use of the formal principles which are dictated by the nature of musical materials.

The symphonic poem is episodic, with the character of the episodes growing out of the program. Musical coherence and variety is secured by the introduction of new and the recurrence of already familiar thematic material.

"Les Préludes" begins, after two soft plucked notes on the tonic, with a melodic line containing the motive which, in various guises, will unify the whole work:

As the first episode proceeds, Liszt's method of theme transformation, by which his basic motive is subjected to numerous variations, will become clear. The original motive is given numerous forms:

This process of theme transformation carries the music to the broad, flowing melodic line in the violoncellos and second violins, a melody which later appears as a horn solo:

This melody prepares the way for a new episode, in which Liszt marks the melody "expressive but tranquil." Here another motive appears:

The music based on this motive grows in intensity, rises to a climax, and subsides very quietly into a statement in the flutes of the original motive:

A third episode begins with the original motive, combined with chromatic scale passages for the violoncellos:

This episode grows in loudness and intensity as the motive appears in the trumpets and trombones:

The agitation increases as Liszt calls for the music to be "tempestoso" and "molto agitato," and the original motive is turned upside down:

This third episode reaches a thunderous climax in which several previous transformations of the thematic material are to be heard. As it comes to an end, the oboe sounds a familiar melodic line:

The fourth episode is a remarkable example of Liszt's tone-color imagination. With only very slight reminiscence of former subject matter at first, but with a consummate use of instrumental effects, he composed music without which Hollywood could hardly show white birches reflected in quiet water. Liszt composed long before the cinema was imagined, too soon for his music to be protected by the copyright laws.

As this episode proceeds, the violins come in unobtrusively with the melodic figure that was characteristic of the second episode:

This familiar melody grows in breadth and strength until it is finally interrupted by the trumpet call:

The reiterated trumpet call is the signal for a tremendous display of musical energy which leads to the fifth and final episode.

The final episode is announced by the horns and trumpets, which play, at a different speed and with new dynamic quality, the familiar thematic material:

Again many of the already familiar transformations of the theme appear, almost in the manner of the recapitulation in the sonata form, but now surrounded by maximum activity of all the orchestra. The flowing theme of the second episode becomes a march:

At the end the original theme is heard in its most energetic transformations, played by the noisiest instruments and surrounded by a mighty fabric of tone from the whole orchestra.

This description of what tones do in "Les Préludes" should make clear the fact that this music has form—its own form. How does it correspond to its program? Listening to the music, we have found that it divides readily into five episodes. Each episode doubtless represented a part of the program to the composer:

Episode I: "Enchanted dawn"
Episode II: "First throbs of happiness"
(The first two episodes are sometimes regarded as a unit.)
Episode III: "Storms whose violent blasts"
Episode IV: "Oblivion in . . . rural life"
Episode V: "The trumpet sound[s] . . . in the struggle complete self-realization" is found.

RICHARD STRAUSS: "DON JUAN"

Strauss describes "Don Juan" as a "tone poem according to Nikolaus Lenau for large orchestra." He quotes part of Lenau's poem opposite the first page of the music:

A magic realm, illimited, eternal,
Of gloried woman,—loveliness supernal!
Fain would I, in the storm of stressful bliss,
Expire upon the last one's lingering kiss!
    Through every realm, O friend, would wing my flight,
Wherever Beauty blooms, kneel down to each,
And, if for one brief moment, win delight!

.   .   .   .

I flee from surfeit and from rapture's cloy,
Keep fresh for Beauty service and employ,
Grieving the One, that All I may enjoy.
My lady's charm today hath breath of spring,
Tomorrow may the air of dungeon bring.
    When with the new love won I sweetly wander,
No bliss is ours upfurbish'd and regilded;
    A different love has This to That one yonder,—
Not up from ruins be my temple builded.
    Yea Love life is, and ever must be now,
Cannot be changed or turned in new direction;
It must expire—here find a resurrection;
    And, if 'tis real, it nothing knows of rue!
Each Beauty in the world is sole, unique;

So must the love be that would Beauty seek!
So long as Youth lives on with pulse afire,
Out to the chase! To victories new aspire!

.   .   .   .   .   .

It was a wond'rous lovely storm that drove me:
Now it is o'er; and calm all round, above me;
   Sheer dead is every wish; all hopes o'ershrouded,—
It was perhaps a flash from heaven descended,
Whose deadly stroke left me with powers ended,
   And all the world, so bright before, o'erclouded;
Yet perchance not! Exhausted is the fuel;
And on the hearth the cold is fiercely cruel.[1]

"Don Juan" was first performed in 1889 at Weimar. It was Strauss's first symphonic poem, and it was destined to introduce a long list of such works for orchestra.

"Don Juan," like "Les Préludes," is constructed as a succession of contrasting and related episodes, which move along without pause between one and another.

EPISODE I

The beginning introduces three rhythmic motives which are to have importance throughout the music:

The first striking melodic line follows very shortly in the violins, with a rushing accompaniment based on the triplet motion of the second introductory motive. Notice that the melodic line is developed from the third introductory motive:

---

[1] Translation by John P. Jackson. Used by permission.

The episode based on this theme continues until a sudden tranquil passage introduces a new motive:

Then follows a bridge passage in which the motives of the first episode are heard again, but in which the new motive continues.

EPISODE II

The second episode, in distinct contrast to the first, moves very quietly, with its motive, already heard in the previous transition, in the solo violin:

As the music of this episode broadens, its motive takes on fuller form and becomes part of a sweeping melodic line— even of a polyphonic fabric in which the motive is heard in imitation:

This second episode moves through a broad climax to a quiet close which is disturbed by two appearances in the violoncellos, against dissonant harmonies, of the three measures with which the piece began. The woodwinds then take up the same three measures, and the music moves to the next episode.

EPISODE III

This episode is based on the material of Episode I, treated similarly, but somewhat more briefly.

EPISODE IV

The beginning of the fourth episode is marked by the sudden disappearance of the theme of the first:

Immediately the violas and violoncellos sing a new melodic line which contains a motive that will appear repeatedly as accompaniment in this section:

Appearances of this melody are separated by a syncopated figure in the flute and by rhythmic reminders of the theme of the first and third episodes:

motives from first and third episodes:

After this rather fragmentary beginning the chief theme of this episode appears in the oboe:

EPISODE V

The fifth episode begins with the entry, after a sudden increase of volume, of a new theme, given out by all four French horns:

The theme of the preceding episode makes one agitated appearance, in a different guise, before the second appearance of the new theme:

After this single reference to the mood of the preceding episode, the new theme takes complete control of the music. It brings with it, however, continual reference to the three motives of the introduction:

EPISODE VI

Strauss marks this episode *giocoso*—jocose, mirthful. Here bits of new melodic material and references to former themes follow each other in what might almost be called a kind of musical disarray. Try to hear the following short themes:

The climax of this episode subsides into a reminiscence of the themes of Episodes II and IV:

Notice how the theme of the fourth episode breaks down and loses its identity as it appears here.

EPISODE VII

The final episode, the seventh, enters with the familiar motives of the introduction. Instead of an immediate statement of the theme of the first episode the music seems still

to carry the weight, the downward pull, of one of the motives of the sixth episode:

Very soon, however, the theme of the first and third episodes
returns, and is followed by the theme of the fifth episode.
It is important to notice that here these two most important
themes appear in the same episode. The music rushes on to a
tremendous climax and ends with a complete silence.

CODA

After the silence that concludes the last episode, the music
begins very quietly, with no motion except a fluttering
tremolo in the violins, on the minor chord of the subdominant. This complete change of pace and subject matter concludes the music.

Our discussion of this music began with a quotation of
the poem which the composer quotes as his program. Thus
far, however, we have been making the acquaintance of the
music without attempting to connect the two. What have
we heard?

For "Don Juan" it is helpful and not at all difficult to

construct the kind of map which we have already used. Assigning letters to the episodes gives the following diagram:

EPISODE I

A

Introductory motives:

1.

2.

3.

Theme:

EPISODE II

B

Motive out of which theme grows:

EPISODE III

A

EPISODE IV

C

Motive of accompaniment:

Theme:

EPISODE V

D

(A)

Theme:

Recurrence in accompaniment of motives from episodes which have been marked with letter *A*.

EPISODE VI

E

Numerous motives:

EPISODE VII

A

Motives and themes of *A* and *D*.

CODA

Bringing these letters together gives a form very much like a rondo:

A B A C D(A) E(D) A Coda

If the listener can grasp a musical substitution that grows out of the program and can accept the theme of *A* and the theme of *D* as representing two aspects of the same thing, there is no difficulty at all in hearing this music as a rondo of seven sections:

A B A C A* D A* Coda

The composer has a right to expect the listener to give his work as careful attention as this; yet a real hearing has no more than begun.

What do these episodes mean in relation to the program? The beginning theme, the theme substituted for it later, and the motives growing out of them must be understood as representing Don Juan. Not only do they become associated in the listener's mind with this character, but they depict, by their motion and tensions, the flow of Don Juan's emotional reactions to his experiences. Thus Don Juan himself is the subject of four episodes. The first two intervening episodes create, by the kind of motion, tone-color, and thematic material in them, an impression so decidedly contrasted to the brusque, often tempestuous qualities of Don Juan's music that it is natural to connect them with the feminine elements of the Lenau poem. The tentative beginnings of these episodes and their dissonant, unmelodious endings are illuminating, as is also the change in character from the thematic material of the first to that of the second.

The substitution of Don Juan themes after the second feminine episode is a stroke of genius. Notice particularly the difference in pace, direction, and weight—loudness, tone-color, range—between these two themes:

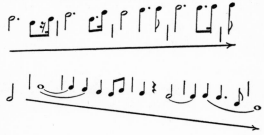

Coming after the second Don Juan theme, the sixth episode speaks for itself, with its several jocose brief subepisodes and the slight reminiscences of the two former feminine episodes which occur at its close. No verbal explanation is needed for the final Don Juan episode, in which the dashing quality of the first Don Juan theme is caught with difficulty and the coarser substitute theme is used; from a hysterical climax it collapses into silence. Finally, there can be no difficulty in connecting the strange harmony, the absence of motion, and the use of the low resonances of the orchestra with the words:

> . . . Exhausted is the fuel;
> And on the hearth the cold is fiercely cruel.

The listener will meet many other symphonic poems as his musical vista broadens. Always he should approach them first as music. No program can explain music which has not been completely heard.

RECORDINGS

| Liszt | "Les Préludes" | Victor M-453 |
| Strauss | "Don Juan" | Victor M-351 |

Chapter 20

WAGNER: ACT I OF
"THE VALKYRIE"

THE span of Wagner's life covered most of the nineteenth century: 1813-1883. His music dramas, for him and for many of his listeners, spanned the whole area of human thought and emotion. Whether Wagner was right in his own evaluation of his work need not trouble us here, but it is certain that music lovers in ever-increasing numbers are finding that his music speaks to them.

Wagner's plans were vast and his ability to realize them extraordinary. No other composer has brought such a complex array of aims and resources to his work, and a listener needs considerable information to appreciate it.

Wagner was not only the musician, but also the philosopher, playwright, and poet of his works, which were conceived as dramas to be played on the stage, with all that poetry, costume, setting, music, and actors could contribute to the total effect. His use of music was governed, aside from the qualities of his own genius, by two ideas to which he often gave expression. They concerned the relation, first, of the theater to society and, second, of music to drama.

Wagner felt that the theater could be a great unifying institution for any society that wanted it to be. He was sure that from the stage, with a work of art as the vehicle, ideas that would make for general social solidarity, loyalty, and well-being could be disseminated. He looked back with nostalgia to the part played by the theater in the ancient Greek city state and craved the same influence for the theater of the nineteenth century.

The ideal relation between music and drama constantly occupied Wagner's mind. He wished to utilize the power of music to move the listener, and at the same time he sought for music the function of another language which should comment on the text and action of the stage drama. He cited the part played by the chorus of the ancient Greek drama—discussion of character, examination of motives underlying speech and action on the stage, implications of the drama that were to be recalled or foreseen—a kind of running psychological commentary on what is going on on the stage. Music, Wagner was sure, could fulfill a like function in connection with drama.

Much of the drama of human relationships proceeds beyond physical observation—in the emotions, in men's souls. Wagner felt that the symphonies of Beethoven dealt with drama of that kind. Might not music drama be the true successor to the Beethoven symphony, by restoring to the operatic stage the part of the total drama that action and gesture not only fail to depict, but may even, by themselves, destroy?

Wagner's musical problem was hardly less acute than that of a composer wishing to substitute the symphonic poem for the symphony. He solved it by directly associating powerful thematic material with characters, incidents, and properties in such a way that when it was heard again, the thematic material would suggest the original association. These short, terse musical motives, in their relation to the drama, are known as leading motives (*Leitmotiven*). They are used with all the emotional shading that the processes of variation, development, and transformation can give them. Woven through the complex fabric of voices and orchestra, they carry the emotional line of the drama. For Wagner, music was above all else "the language of emotion."

The Valkyrie (*Die Walküre*) is the second of the cycle of four dramas, *The Ring of the Nibelungen* (*Der Ring des Nibelungen*). The whole cycle, consisting of *The Rhinegold* (*Das Rheingold*), *The Valkyrie, Siegfried,* and *The Twilight of the Gods* (*Götterdämmerung*), deals with the struggle for mastery and power between the gods who live above the earth, the giants who live on the earth, and the Nibelungen who live beneath the earth. In the struggle the dignities and common failings not only of humanity but of codes and institutions take their part. Many listeners find in the cycle an immense allegory of the life of the nineteenth century, but the realization of any such significance must wait for more than introductory acquaintance.[1]

The first drama, *The Rhinegold,* ends with the procession of the gods, led by the one-eyed Wotan,[2] into their newly built stronghold, Walhall. The triumphal entry, however, is not without misgivings. Wotan, hiring the giants to build the place, had promised to give them Freia, the goddess of immortality, as payment. He had made this pledge only because he had been assured by Loge, the god of deceit, that he would not need to fulfill it. Indeed the gods could hardly survive without immortality. Loge finds a way to save Freia. He leads Wotan to the cavern home of Alberich, the master of

[1] See George Bernard Shaw, *The Perfect Wagnerite*.
[2] The English version of Wagnerian proper nouns is taken from the complete vocal score as published by G. Schirmer. German *w* has not been changed; it should be pronounced like English *v*.

the Nibelungen, and there by a deception which is not at all godlike they steal Alberich's gold, even to the symbols of its power, the Tarnhelm, which is the cap of invisibility, and the Ring. They justify their theft by reminding themselves that Alberich himself had originally stolen the gold from the Rhine maidens and that he had not only forsworn love in stealing it but used the gold to enslave his fellows.

Wotan and Loge do not get the gold, however, without a strong intimation of what the theft is to cost them. Alberich curses the gold and threatens that he will get it back; when he does he will use its power, as symbolized by the Ring, to destroy the gods. The giants, coming for their pay, are not satisfied to take the gold as a substitute for Freia until it has been piled high enough to hide her completely from their sight. This takes even the Ring, which Wotan had hoped to keep. But he could not give up immortality for a distant threat to his existence. The curse of the gold begins to work. The giants quarrel over its division. One of them kills the other and then has to bury the gold in a cavern and change himself into a dragon, with the aid of the Tarnhelm, to guard it. As the gods enter Walhall, then, they are moving into a castle which has cost them a threat to their very existence. If Alberich can get the gold from the giant, the gods will be destroyed. Wotan must find some way to lift that threat.

Between *The Rhinegold* and *The Valkyrie* considerable time has passed. Wotan has been busy with his problem. As a temporary defense he has created a race of warrior maidens. They are the Valkyries, and it is their duty to carry to Walhall the heroes who fall on the battlefields of earth. The heroes will partake of the immortality of the gods and will act as an armed guard for the castle. But this army, re-

cruited by the warrior maidens, is only a temporary expedi-
ent; to be free of his difficulty Wotan must find a way to
return the gold to its original owners, the Rhine maidens.
Wotan cannot do it himself. By the same moral code that
he has pledged himself to support he is prevented from again
stealing the gold. But if he can find one who is free from the
laws that bind even the gods, one who, out of his own freedom and fearlessness, will kill the dragon and restore the
gold, his problem will be solved.

Wotan tries to create such a hero, or at least a race from
which the hero may spring. He goes to the earth and, as
Wälse, becomes the father of the race—half god, half human
—known as the Wälsungs. The first generation of that race
are Siegmund and Sieglinde. Act I of *The Valkyrie* takes up
their story.

The Prelude begins with the motive of the storm which
will be the background of the opening of the act:

The Storm

The ebb and flow of the storm motive, punctuated by brilliant flashes from the high woodwind and brass instruments,
bring the Prelude to a close.

As the curtain rises it discloses a room built around the
trunk of a great tree. The storm is heard continuing outside.
As Siegmund stumbles through the door, the orchestra announces him with a motive characterized by its descending
motion:

Siegmund's Fatigue

Siegmund asks whose house he has entered and, as he sinks to
the floor exhausted, says that here he must rest. As the or-

chestra continues with the motives of the storm and Siegmund's fatigue, Sieglinde enters, sees Siegmund as a total
stranger, and is anxious over his identity and condition. The
orchestra describes her anxiety and compassion with the motive of Sieglinde's compassion:

Sieglinde's Compassion

Siegmund asks for a drink of water, and as Sieglinde brings
it, the orchestra develops the Siegmund and Sieglinde motives. Almost imperceptibly, as Siegmund and Sieglinde
watch each other, the orchestra introduces two very important motives, which are to be associated with the growing
attraction of Siegmund and Sieglinde to each other. The
first is the motive of brother and sister affection, for although they are strangers and unaware of their relationship,
they are actually twin brother and sister, the children of
Wälse:

Brother and Sister Affection

This motive is heard twice and is followed immediately by
the very important love motive:

Love

Notice that the love motive actually includes part of the
brother and sister motive:

The drama continues to develop as Siegmund inquires where he is and who has taken care of him. Sieglinde answers that she is the wife of Hunding and that this is Hunding's house. Siegmund answers that he has been in battle and is now weaponless and exhausted by his flight from his foe. The motives of Siegmund's fatigue, Sieglinde's compassion, brother and sister affection, and love are woven into the orchestral fabric which accompanies this part of the scene.

After a tender orchestral interlude Siegmund starts to leave, saying that he always has bad luck and will go before he brings it to Sieglinde. Notice here the new form of the compassion motive, which can be heard at the beginning of the Victor record 8933-B (Schirmer vocal score, page 13, third and fourth lines):

One of Wagner's most felicitous uses of the leading motive follows immediately. Sieglinde asks Siegmund who pursues him that he must leave, and he replies, twice, that it is bad luck that follows him. Each phrase of his answer is preceded by a long-held note in the orchestra, each time rising and increasing in intensity. After the second phrase the long-held note is heard again, as though to introduce another phrase from Siegmund. Instead, however, the orchestra subsides into a gentle reiteration of the love motive:

Love motive

A moment later Sieglinde tells Siegmund that he may as well remain. He cannot bring ill fortune to a place where it has already made its home. Part of the phrase which Sieglinde sings is the brother and sister motive:

Then bide thou here!   *Ill fate thou cans't not bring*   *here,*
So blei - be hier   Nicht bringst du · Un - heil da - hin,

This is followed immediately by the announcement of another important motive, the song of the Wälsungs. This is one of several motives associated with this race; its solemn upward swing and fall back to a position which gives it a feeling of incompletion hint at its peculiar significance:

Song of the Wälsungs

This new motive is interwoven with the motive of compassion, and as it moves along at the bottom of the music, it almost imperceptibly changes, first to the love motive and finally, at the very end of the scene, to the motive of Siegmund's fatigue (Schirmer vocal score, page 15).

The second scene begins with the distant announcement of the approach of Hunding, Sieglinde's husband. The Hunding motive is gruff and requires a tone-color which Wagner supplied by using the so-called Wagnerian tubas:

Hunding

As Hunding enters he looks inquiringly at Siegmund. Sieglinde and then Siegmund try to explain the presence of the stranger. The storm motive is heard momentarily, and as Hunding settles himself for his evening meal, the Hunding motive again.

As Sieglinde prepares the meal, Hunding watches her and the strange guest and remarks upon their resemblance to each other. The orchestra prepares for his remark with the compassion and the brother and sister motives. At the end of his remark the orchestra whispers a motive which, in *The Rhinegold*, has been associated with Wotan, who, as Wälse, was the father of Siegmund and Sieglinde. It symbolizes his spear, upon the handle of which had been carved Wotan's promise to uphold the law:

Wotan's Spear (and Promise)

Thus the orchestral fabric hints at what is known to none of the characters on the stage.

The scene continues as Siegmund is persuaded to tell what he knows of his own background. He does not tell his name, but recounts that he called his father Wolfe. He was born a twin. But the Neidings, at mention of whom the Hunding motive is heard in the orchestra, had murdered his mother and carried off his twin sister. Let him be called Wehwalt the Wölfing,[3] son of Wolfe, says Siegmund. Hunding has heard dark rumors of Wolfe and Wölfing and wants to hear more. Siegmund tells of the battle in which his father was lost to sight; he does not know where his father is. At this point (Victor 8935-A; Schirmer vocal score, page 26), the orchestra answers Sieglinde's question as to the whereabouts of Wolfe, which Siegmund himself cannot answer. This answer is the powerful motive that stands for both Wotan and Walhall:

Wotan-Walhall

---

[3] A characteristic Wagnerian play on words: *Weh* = woe, *walten* = to govern; *Wehwalt* = ruled by woe; *Wölfing* = diminutive of wolf.

Siegmund goes on to explain that after his father was lost, he longed for the company of other men and women, but that his ill fortune prevented him from ever making friends. As the recital continues, it is punctuated by the motives of compassion, love, Hunding, and the song of the Wälsungs. Sieglinde finally asks how Siegmund came to be in his present plight.

The answer is fatal, because it shows that Hunding and Siegmund must be deadly enemies. Siegmund had interfered in the marriage of a girl against her will, had fought and killed many of her kinsmen, and had been forced to flee from the rest, of whom Hunding was one. The orchestra supplies a highly effective background by mirroring the ebb and flow of movement in Siegmund's narrative. The motives of Siegmund's fatigue, the storm, and the song of the Wälsungs are used with telling effect. At the end of Siegmund's tale, the orchestra presents a new motive, another motive for the Wälsung race. Notice its resemblance to the Wotan-Walhall motive and its unfinished-sounding conclusion (end of Victor 8935-B; Schirmer vocal score, page 32):

The Wälsungs

Hunding, enraged to find his enemy sheltered in his own house, allows Siegmund hospitality for the night, but challenges him to mortal combat for the morrow. Hunding bids Sieglinde make ready his evening drink and prepares to leave the weaponless Siegmund for the night. As Sieglinde prepares the drink, she watches Siegmund, and the orchestra not only follows her thoughts, but indicates the as yet unrealized relationship of the twin brother and sister. After this little tone poem based on the motives of compassion and of brother and sister affection, Sieglinde tries to direct Siegmund's gaze to the trunk of the tree around which the room is built. At that point (Victor 8936-A; Schirmer vocal score, page 35) the orchestra plays the motive of the sword:

The Sword

Sieglinde puts a sleeping potion in Hunding's drink as she goes out the door. Hunding, after one more threat, leaves, and his motive echoes through the orchestra.

The room darkens to the glow of the hearth as Siegmund sits alone; the final scene of the act is beginning. The music suggests Hunding and the sword. Siegmund remembers that his father had promised him a weapon, to be ready to his hand at his time of greatest need. Surely this is the time. He is a hostage, weaponless, in his enemy's house—a hostage to this beautiful woman whom he has just now met! Notice the form of the love motive here:

He calls on his father, asking for his sword, with music which, later on in this act and again in *Siegfried,* will be connected with the sword under its name of Nothung:

As the fire brightens, Siegmund sees a reflection from the trunk of the tree. The orchestra speaks insistently of the sword, but Siegmund imagines the reflection to be a glance of Sieglinde's lingering in the room after she has gone.

A reminiscence of the motives of Hunding, of the song of the Wälsungs, and of Sieglinde's compassion announce the entrance of Sieglinde, who has come to show Siegmund a weapon. But first she must tell her story, because the weapon and the man who alone shall be able to use it are bound up with her own fate. At her sad, loveless marriage to Hunding a stranger appeared, a stranger who looked at her from only one eye. As she mentions the stranger the orchestra identifies him with the tremendously resonant motive of Wotan-Walhall. As the Wotan-Walhall motive disappears, Sieglinde speaks of the tenderness with which the stranger regarded her. Here is a passage which is Wagner at his greatest:

The orchestra mentions the sword as Sieglinde tells how the stranger thrust his own sword into the trunk of the tree. There it remains; the hero for whom it is intended has not yet been disclosed. Now Sieglinde realizes who the stranger is and for whom the sword was intended. The orchestra makes a powerful crescendo with the Wotan-Walhall and the sword motives as Sieglinde expresses her hope that the hero who shall claim the sword and avenge the shame of her marriage with Hunding has at last arrived.

Siegmund, overcome by Sieglinde's hope and affection, pronounces the oath that weds him to Sieglinde and promises to be her avenger. They embrace, and the mood of the music suddenly changes; the storm is over; spring has come. The storm motive resolves into a gentle introduction to the famous love duet. Siegmund begins with the motive of love and spring:

Notice how Wagner, as this scene proceeds, weaves the motives of love and of brother and sister affection into the fabric, now in the orchestra, now in the voices.

As they become accustomed to the enchantment of their love for each other, the mood of the music changes. Wagner accomplishes this by introducing a new motive which we may indicate as the joy of love (Victor 8938-B; Schirmer vocal score, page 61):

Notice the exhilarating effect of the use of only the first part of this motive in leading to a reiteration of the love motive:

As the lovers look at each other more closely, Sieglinde's memory begins to bring back sounds and pictures. She seems to have seen before what she sees now, and the orchestra gives forth the Wotan-Walhall motive. The surface of the brook that mirrored her face showed her the face she now sees as she gazes at Siegmund; the voice she now hears, which she seems to remember faintly from her childhood, is the same voice that echoed back from her own call in the forest. The light of the eyes she now sees reminds her of the earlier stranger who brought the sword. Is the newcomer's name really Wehwalt? Notice the echoing use of the brother and sister motive, the suggestion of the Wälsung motive, and the use of the sword and Wotan-Walhall motives.

No longer, Siegmund agrees, can he be called Wehwalt—Sieglinde has changed all that—she may give him a more fitting name. But was his father really Wolfe? No, not except to cowardly foxes; he was really Wälse.

This is the news that Sieglinde had been awaiting. It is Siegmund the Wälsung who stands before her, the one for whom the sword in the tree was intended. As the sword motive resounds in the orchestra, Siegfried grasps the sword and draws it from the tree.

At this point Wagner uses a motive new to this act to make a powerful reference. In *The Rhinegold*, Alberich, in stealing the gold from the Rhine maidens, renounced love. Wagner uses the motive of that renunciation here as Siegmund proclaims that his great love will drive him to heroic deeds and to death:

Renunciation of Love

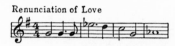

Then he names the sword Nothung, while we hear the Nothung motive with which he called on his father at the beginning of the scene.

As Siegmund offers the sword as a bridal gift, the two lovers pledge, as brother and sister and as bride and bridegroom, that the race of the Wälsungs shall flourish forever. This final moment builds to a tremendous climax with a musical fabric in which the first half of the Wälsung motive, the sword motive, the joy of love motive, and the love motive are all woven together. Notice the acceleration produced by the different forms in which the love motive appears:

As the listener masters the complex musical fabric of this act, he will undoubtedly want to refer to music and text. The following tables will lighten the difficulty of keeping his place. For keep his place he must if he wishes to partake of the true riches of a Wagnerian music drama.

RECORDINGS

Wagner	*Die Walküre*, Act I	Victor M-245

RECORD SIDE	PAGES IN SCHIRMER VOCAL SCORE
8932-A	1-6 first measure of fourth staff
B	6-9 middle of third staff
8933-A	9-13 beginning of third staff
B	9-16 middle of second staff
8934-A	16-20 middle of third staff
B	20-24 end of second staff
8935-A	24-28 first measure of page
B	28-32 next to last measure of third staff
8936-A	32-36 end of first staff
B	36-39 middle of second staff
8937-A	39-44 first measure of second staff
B	44-49 next to last measure of third staff
8938-A	49-58 first measure of page
B	58-63 beginning of fourth staff
8939-A	63-70 first measure of page
B	70-77 end of Act I

The Storm

Siegmund's Fatigue

Sieglinde's Compassion

Brother and Sister Affection

Love

Song of the Wälsungs

Hunding

Wotan's Spear (and Promise)

Wotan-Walhall

The Wälsungs

The Sword

Nothung

Wäl - se

Love and Spring

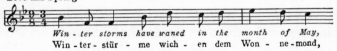

Win - ter storms have waned in the month of May,
Win - ter - stür - me wich - en dem Won - ne - mond,

Joy of Love

O sweet - est en - chant - ment
O süs - ses - te Won - ne

Renunciation of Love

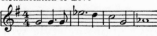

271

Chapter 21

A FAMOUS SYMPHONY:
BRAHMS'S FIRST

JOHANNES BRAHMS'S First Symphony was first performed in 1876 when its composer was forty-three years old. Brahms once wrote that "in these days a symphony is no joke." He began to sketch this symphony in 1862; that he worked on it over a period of fourteen years indicates how seriously he took it. The length of time a composer spends on a symphony is not, however, a matter of great importance to the listener unless there is a connection between it and the problems involved in listening to the music. In this case there is such a connection. Brahms explored the implications of his subject matter so thoroughly that the resulting musical fabric demands of the listener an effort of hearing and understanding comparable to the care the composer used in writing it. Through this complex but magnificent musical fabric the listener may come to feel and understand the warm-hearted message of its composer, if he will but give himself the opportunity.

To penetrate Brahms's First Symphony is no easy undertaking. Hearing and understanding must reinforce each other. The listener is advised to make two sorts of approach. First, get used to the sheer sound of the symphony. After a few hearings Brahms's idiom or style will begin to seem familiar, and landmarks within the music will catch the attention. Then use, for one or two hearings, the first, sketchy analysis which follows. The main themes of each movement will by then have become clear, and the listener will be ready to perceive the relationships to which the second, much more detailed analysis will serve as a guide. Finally, hear the symphony over and over until even the detailed analysis in this chapter begins to seem sketchy.

The first guide follows.

FIRST MOVEMENT

Introduction (slow):

First theme (change to faster time):

Second theme:

Closing theme:

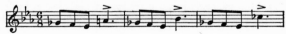

SECOND MOVEMENT

A somewhat complex ternary form in which section A has two motto themes:

THIRD MOVEMENT

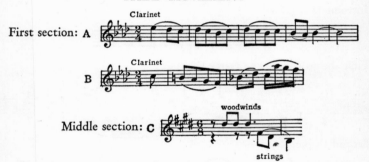

FOURTH MOVEMENT

Introduction:

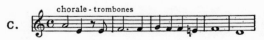

First theme:

Second theme:

Closing episode:

After the listener has heard this thematic material often enough to anticipate its appearance in the various movements, let him proceed to the following more detailed analysis.

FIRST MOVEMENT

The first movement may be heard as a rather complex sonata form. It begins with a slow, sustained introduction which grows out of the lines of the first two measures:

Try to hear the important motives contained in these early measures. First the three-note chromatic ascending figure:

Second, the counterpart of the first, the descending line
which contains a three-note chromatic fall:

Then, the rhythmic figure with which the rising line ends:

As the introduction proceeds, Brahms momentarily releases the tension of these lines moving toward and away
from the pounded reiteration of the bass instruments; but
that release only leads to another statement, on the dominant level, of the music of the beginning.

At the moment when the music changes from the rather
slow pulse of the introduction to the rapid movement, the
woodwinds sound the essence of the whole introduction:

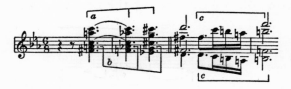

The first violins then give out what is usually called the
first theme. Even a first hearing should show that part of
the introduction remains as an accompanying line in the
violoncellos and bassoons:

Brahms has now given himself at least five motives with which to continue. His use of them will be complex. To follow him is a test for any listener. Almost immediately he begins to hide the ascending and descending chromatic lines in seemingly novel material:

The passage which follows gives the listener a hint of the processes by which Brahms is going to carry this music forward. The figure that the violoncellos had before is given to the higher instruments, and the low parts continue with another version of motive *b*:

The relationship of motive *d* with motive *b* is soon established. It was first heard against *a* and *c*.

The careful listener will soon discern that the passage cited above contains all five of the motives. This complexity of texture is characteristic of Brahms. As the first-theme section continues, many other similar passages will occur. The result is a fabric of great richness.

The preparation for the second theme is made during the first quiet passage of the Allegro. The theme itself is not new material, but a new combination of motives previously heard; compare with the first theme (page 276). Here motive *a* is heard above the rest of the fabric, while motive *d* is below. Motives *c* and *e* do not appear:

This statement of the second theme is followed immediately by a lovely melodic line in the oboe. Although this oboe melody at first hearing seems to bear very little resemblance to any of the motives previously heard, the listener's mind will in time perceive a characteristic Brahmsian relationship to motive *b:*

In the very quiet accompaniment to this part of the second theme, the music opens in diverging lines which are reminiscent of the more familiar appearances of motives *a* and *b*.

The quietness of the second-theme section is broken by the

marked entrance in the violas, against a background of
plucked chords, of a short figure out of which will grow a
theme of such strength that it must be thought of as a
closing theme. This short figure is actually a new form of
motive *b:*

At this point, with a burst of tremendous vitality, Brahms
achieves a remarkable recombination of already familiar
motives. The violins play a melodic line which is a new form
of motives *a* and *b:*

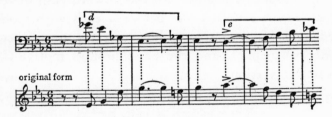

Simultaneously, the lower instruments play an inversion of
the line in which motives *d* and *e* were first heard:

Try to hear how these go together:

Before the development section is reached, the closing theme
receives another interesting inversion:

This description of the subject matter of the first movement should furnish the listener with a guide to further discovery. He must penetrate a complex musical fabric. Brahms asks his listeners to accept musical relationships which tax their perceptions. Many instances are apparent in the exposition; the development presents many more. Only one will be cited here. The listener will enjoy finding more for himself.

The development begins with the upward rush of motive *d,* which recurs several times before it ends with motive *e.* Immediately after motive *e,* however, the music becomes suddenly very quiet, and the bassoon sings motive *d* in a much slower version:

With the last part (*d*¹) of this new version of the motive as a pattern, the music develops an interesting version of motive *a:*

SECOND MOVEMENT

The second movement begins with a very simple and un-obtrusive statement of three motives:

Motive *b* will be heard as a kind of motto throughout the movement. A submotive will be derived from *b,* and the derivation will be reinforced by the fact that it contains the rhythmic figure common to all three motives:

This will be heard as the heart of a later melody.

Motive *c* will be recognized immediately as a reminiscence of motive *a* of the first movement—the upward thrust of three semitones. The reminiscence becomes clearer when the listener notices the presence here again of the downward counterpart, called motive *b* in the first movement:

The music grows from these motives toward the lovely melodic line which is first given out by the oboe. Notice that this melody contains the reference to motive *b:*

One statement of this melody suffices for the beginning. The movement continues with a long, florid melodic line carried by the violins which also contains references to the motive which is a memory from the first movement:

The working out of this melodic line fills the middle section of the movement.

Motives *b* and *c* announce the appearance of the final section in which the melody that originally appeared in the oboe is given to French horn and solo violin. Here Brahms brings all of the material of the movement together into a magnificent orchestral fabric which furnishes a background for the soaring sweetness of the solo violin.

THIRD MOVEMENT

Brahms marks the third movement *un poco allegretto e grazioso*—rather lively and gracefully flowing. In form this movement is derived from the earlier minuet, although its rhythm is not that of the minuet and there are some deviations in form. The melodic material of the first subsection appears immediately in the clarinet. Notice that Brahms uses one of his characteristic methods of melodic treatment. No sooner has the five-measure statement been heard than it is heard again in an inverted form:

The subsection is completed by a kind of answer based on the following material:

After a repeat, with changed tone-color and a slightly different ending, a new melody from the clarinet announces the next subsection:

This subsection contains and ends with references to the material of the previous subsection. Thus the movement so far bears considerable resemblance to the part of the earlier minuet which is the minuet proper:

‖: *a* :‖ *b′* *a* ‖

The repeat of subsection *a* was different from the original statement, and the subsection *ba* was not repeated.

A change of time and rhythm, of key, of tone-color, and of thematic material marks the appearance of what would be the trio in the older minuet. This section, which is repeated, grows entirely out of the thematic material first announced by the woodwinds and strings:

The return of the first section is presaged by the use of the first measure of the original thematic material in two forms:

Notice how the woodwinds carry over into this section some of the characteristic rhythms of the middle section. Notice, too, how Brahms avoids the literal inversion of his thematic material. The clarinet theme is answered, not by its exact inversion, but by a variation of that inversion:

The movement closes with a coda based on the material of the middle section.

FOURTH MOVEMENT

The final movement of Brahms's First Symphony is one of the monuments of symphonic literature. Many listeners are on the alert for the great "tune" of its first theme and rather endure most of the rest of its broad expanses. It is difficult to understand, however, how the message of the whole symphony can be grasped unless this movement eventually comes to mean more than a series of brackets around a magnificent melody. Here, as never before, the listener must follow the fabric of Brahms's music in intimate detail before he can hope to understand it. The composer did not spend fourteen years on this work in waste motion.

The movement begins with a slow introduction. The immediate statement of thematic material is rich in motives:

As the music proceeds, Brahms will utilize every implication of this beginning that fits into his plan. Those implications eventually become clear; the process may be hastened by an analysis. The downward flow of the first three notes is twice echoed by the woodwinds:

The most important motive of this beginning may be said to contain several submotives:

Notice that the woodwind figure has a simultaneous variation of submotive *a1*, which is labeled *a1'*, and that submotive *a2* has two versions:

When these submotives are translated into terms of motion we get the following picture:

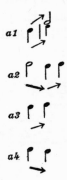

The utilization of these various motives becomes evident immediately as the music proceeds. After the original statement of motive *a* the violins continue with submotives:

The pizzicato or plucked passage that follows is a kind of musical "moreover," discussing the motion of the beginning—slow-starting, but with a tremendously vital upward rush inherent in it. After the first pizzicato passage the music of the beginning is heard again, now at the tonic level instead of the dominant, and with motive *a* below and motive *b* above the chromatic motion. Following the second pizzicato passage, for two measures Brahms pits the descent of motive *b* against upward-rushing scales:

The scales introduce a complex pattern in which all the motions of the original motives are discussed, with the emphasis on *a1*:

The climax of this passage is followed by a fluttery disappearance of a very rapid version of motive *b*, accompanied, however, by an equally rapid version of motive *a2*:

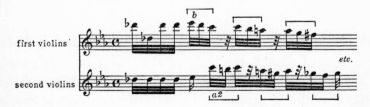

From this passage the music subsides to the second part of the introduction. Here the music has a slightly more rapid

pulse—*più andante*—and it is in the major. The thematic
material is the simple but powerful horn-call theme:

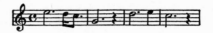

After this theme has been transferred to the flute, the trombones and bassoons announce one of the most famous short
passages in modern symphonic literature, the one-phrase
chorale:

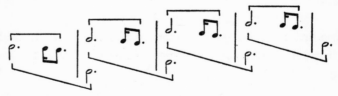

Following this chorale, the horn theme is heard again.
Notice how it is given increased intensity by the manner in
which Brahms treats its first measure as a motive for succes-
sive entrances. This process by which the composer emphasizes a particular motive within a theme is important. The
motive will appear again:

This music comes to a quiet close on the dominant, and after
a moment of silence, the body of the movement begins with
its magnificent first theme. The listener must not fail to
notice that **the beginning of the theme melody is motive
a from the introduction,** with all the possibilities for development that have already been hinted:

As the theme proceeds, Brahms takes care to point to another motive:

The bridge to the second theme becomes apparent when the music begins a more fragmentary discussion of the thematic material. The process of the introduction with regard to motive *a* begins anew:

The bridge ends with one statement of the horn theme from the introduction, immediately followed by the second theme:

Brahms's ingenuity is nowhere better illustrated than with this second theme. As a theme it has its own individuality. As an integral part of this movement and this symphony it is a recombination of submotives *a4* and *a3*, in their major key version, from the introduction:

As one becomes acquainted with this second theme, its growth from these two submotives will become increasingly clear:

decoration of first four notes   decorated inversions of first four notes

The second theme, with its accompanying figure growing out of motive *b* of the introduction, develops into a lovely melody in the oboe and finally leads to a closing episode based on two motives:

Notice the appearance of submotive *a1* in both of these motives. Notice, too, that they both appear in conjunction with other motives from the introduction.

Our discussion has covered the thematic material for this movement. It should be clear that because of the very nature of the thematic material, the process of development begins with the statements of the themes. It is not an exaggeration to say that the whole of the main body of the movement is a development, an expansion into a sonatalike form, of the material which is first heard in the introduction. Because of this fact, Brahms does not give us a long development section followed by the traditional restatement of the first-theme part of the recapitulation. At the point where the development section would normally occur, we hear what is actually the only recapitulation of the first theme. Between this restatement of the first theme and the normal recapitulation of the second theme a broad development takes place —sufficient for Brahms's purpose and sufficient, too, to give a masterly logic to his procedure. This development adds its weight to the intensity of Brahms's interest in discussing what all the thematic material has been hinting, the tremendous upward-thrusting vitality of the basic motives of the music.

At the close of the development the horn-call theme is heard in a very rapid form:

This in turn changes to the original form, which leads to the return of the second theme.

As the music approaches the final closing episode, motive *a* appears in imitation, accompanied by a figure which, first heard in the exposition, grew out of the inversion of the decorated version of the second theme:

This leads to an accelerated use of submotive *a1* which, with the start of the faster coda, becomes a new form of submotive *a2*:

Here in the coda it has this form:

This rushing form of submotive *a2*, which by now is a reminder of one aspect of the first theme, piles up until its intensity expands into a gigantic statement of the chorale of the introduction. From this magnificent climax the music moves rapidly to the end of the movement. In so doing it makes use of the triplet motive which was associated, not only in the exposition of this movement, but also in the first movement, with a closing episode.

The listener who lingers over Brahms's First Symphony to become intimately familiar with it deserves, but hardly needs, a third analysis. He hardly needs it, because, if he has reached some independence in his listening, he has been making it for himself. What does this music mean?

Begin to think of the music of this symphony in terms of tension and motion. The introduction to the first movement outlines the drama of the whole work. Against the thunderous reiteration in the bass, against, too, the steady fall of the inner voices, the violins, through consonance and dissonance, soar upward. As the movement gathers momentum that upward thrust pervades every theme. It gathers to itself the new motives of other themes. No matter what momentary emphasis or appealing form the contradictions of that upward thrust may take, its strength and vitality are sufficient to bring the movement to a triumphant close. On a more complex level and with heightened dramatic intensity, we find here the emotional line that was traced in our analysis of Beethoven's First Symphony.

The second movement, by moving immediately into a distant key and a quiet, lyrical mood, seems to attempt to take the symphony and the listener as far from the intensity of the first movement as possible. But the attempt is not wholly successful. The strength of the first movement is not long in returning, though reminiscently, and with its return the pulse of the music quickens. Yet the movement continues the attempt to reconcile the loveliness of its own themes with the remembered vitality. At the end the two prove not incompatible.

The third movement is really an intermezzo, a moment of relief between more important matters. The mood of great drama cannot be sustained too long. This rather quiet and gracious movement releases the tension. But Brahms has calculated the amount of the release. This intermezzo has its somber moments, its small tensions, and it ends with a quiet abruptness that asks for renewed attention.

With the final movement comes a return to the conflict between the upward thrust and downward pull of the first movement. The themes are new, but again they embody a dualism from which release can come only through the most intense and persuasive analysis and development of the forces involved. The long and unabating process of musical development finally establishes, through passages which are of almost ugly strength, the triumphant message of the symphony.

✦

This discussion of a Brahms symphony needs a footnote reference to one of Brahms's great contemporaries. A music lover will not have achieved a fairly comprehensive acquaintance with great music until he knows Tchaikovsky. If he can really hear Brahms, the utter directness of Tchaikovsky will offer no difficulties. But as he listens to the Fifth or the Sixth Symphony of the Russian master, let him make comparisons of the meaning of this music with that of Brahms. The Tchaikovsky of the last two symphonies composed music in which the same conflicts appear as in the Brahms symphony, but in which the depressing weight inherent in the thematic material overwhelms all other aspects. The final result is in direct contrast to what the music of Brahms achieves. A comparison of the two will help clarify the whole question of musical meanings; it will, moreover, prove with what certainty one may speak of the triumphant message of this Brahms symphony.

RECORDING

Brahms   Symphony No. 1   Victor M-301

Chapter 22

A BACH CANTATA

IN May, 1723, Bach moved his family to the city of Leipzig, where he was to have charge of the music at the St. Thomas Church. For the following Easter, his first in Leipzig, Bach prepared a new cantata. It is known as Cantata No. 4, "Christ lay fast bound in Death's harsh chain" ("Christ lag in Todesbanden").

When the St. Thomas congregation came to church that Easter day, its members brought with them much the same background with regard to church music as could be found among many devout congregations today. They knew the standard hymns or chorales of their church, and they understood that many of those chorales had a special significance in relation to the church calendar. They undoubtedly knew, probably from memory, Martin Luther's great Easter hymn; as youngsters, they had learned it before confirmation; as adults, they began to understand it.

One can easily imagine that many of the good Leipzigers came to church that day with rather eager curiosity about the music they were to hear. Easter is a time for music, and they had within the year secured one of the best musicians of Germany as their cantor. Undoubtedly, too, they had heard from members of the choir and orchestra that some interesting music was in preparation, that they were going to be treated to a new version of the Easter hymn they knew so well.

What did they hear?

The modern listener cannot hope nor should he desire to recapture the mental preparation of Bach's congregation for a first hearing of this cantata. But that audience had one very important qualification; it knew the tune of Luther's hymn. Bach must have counted on that familiarity. If the curiosity of the modern listener is to be satisfied, he too must know the hymn. Fortunately, Bach ended the cantata with the hymn in a simple version, in the singing of which the congregation was probably expected to take part. It is the seventh verse. Turn first to the last two thirds of the last record side and learn it. Learn it so well that you can hum the tune. You are hearing it performed in Spanish by a choir in Barcelona. The performance is slightly shaky in one or two places, but the music is so great that it can withstand an occasional mishap. There is no reason to believe that Bach or any other genuine lover of music would let a slight accident in performance stand between him and the understanding of great music. Here is the music:

Now that the listener has a preliminary acquaintance with the hymn out of which this cantata grew, let us turn to the beginning of the music.

The cantata begins with a short introduction, played by the organ and string orchestra, which Bach calls a Sinfonia. This music was written before the time of either our modern symphony or our symphony orchestra. Bach's use of the word "sinfonia" meant simply that he was writing music for an instrumental ensemble. As the cantata proceeds, it will become increasingly clear that Bach understands his text as a drama, a small religious opera. As a preparation for what is to follow, the Sinfonia has a function similar to that of the operatic overture. The text of the drama begins with the words which give the cantata its title. The music of the chorale begins with a falling inflection:

For the Sinfonia, Bach begins by exploiting that falling inflection:

Notice how the music continues this motion at the bottom as it resolves into the first phrase of the chorale tune at the top. The depressed quality of the beginning of the Sinfonia lasts only until the lift of the first phrase of the tune has made itself felt; after that the free movement of the melodic lines leads to a strong climax.

VERSE I

Christ lay fast bound in Death's harsh chain,
Who for our sins was given.
Now is He raised up again
And brings us Life and Heaven.
Therefore let us joyful be.
Praise God and thank Him heartily
In singing Hallelujah!
Hallelujah!

In this verse, for full chorus, organ, and orchestra, the listener meets a highly complex polyphonic texture. Hearing it is not difficult, however, because all of the melodic lines grow so obviously out of the tune of the chorale. Notice first that the sopranos sing the text of the verse straight through, to the melody of the chorale. But here the melody is in long notes. As the sopranos proceed slowly with the melody, the other parts weave a rich polyphonic web around it. That fabric, even to the details of figuration in the accompaniment, is drawn from the phrase of the melody which is being sung. Thus a complete hearing of this verse must grow out of a phrase-by-phrase analysis.

First phrase:

The other voices enter under the long first note of the phrase, one after the other.

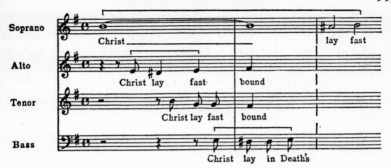

Notice that both alto and bass enter with a melodic line which imitates the first three notes of the chorale tune. After two measures the orchestra develops a short figure from those same three notes—a figure which continues through most of the verse:

This fabric goes on past the soprano statement of the phrase and ends at the point where the next soprano phrase begins.

Second phrase:

For this phrase the other parts are given melodic lines which grow out of the chromaticism of the first two notes of the first phrase, one climbing upward, the other sinking downward:

The polyphonic choral treatment of this phrase ends at the point where the sopranos end it. Another reading of the text will show that the mood changes at the end of the second line. For the third phrase Bach changes the musical mood.

Third phrase:

The third phrase is a repeat, in the chorale, of the first. To continue the soprano part as he has begun it, Bach will use the phrase again, but because the text now speaks of the resurrection, the long-note version is postponed. The melodic phrase is heard first in quicker notes, with a counter melody which describes the motion involved in the text:

Alto, tenor, and bass enter, one after the other, with the chorale phrase before the sopranos sing it in long notes:

Under this soprano phrase the accompaniment turns again to the three-note figure mentioned previously, and the other three voices enter consecutively with a new phrase, which again uses the characteristic three-note motive:

Now is He rais - - ed

Fourth phrase:

In the fourth phrase the treatment is similar to that of the third phrase in postponing the soprano statement of the phrase. The listener should notice how the text, "And brings us Life and Heaven," is reflected in the increased activity of the music. The tenors begin with the choral phrase for the fourth line in quick notes. No sooner have they begun, however, than the altos give out an imitation which is so altered that its first three notes sound like the beginning of the first phrase:

altos

And brings us Life and Hea - ven

tenors

And brings us Life and Hea - ven

Out of this beginning develops the exuberant setting of the word "Heaven":

Hea - - ven

This exuberance continues under the statement of the phrase by the sopranos:

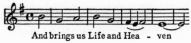

And brings us Life and Hea - ven

Fifth phrase:

The fifth phrase again postpones the soprano statement while the other three voices build up an imitative passage based on the melody of the new phrase. Notice particularly how the music continues to gather energy—how the word "joyful" inspires Bach to write long chains of rapid notes:

As this texture gathers momentum, the sopranos sing the fifth phrase of the chorale tune above it:

A short continuation in the orchestra and organ leads to the music which surrounds the next phrase.

Sixth phrase:

In the sixth phrase, the long-note version of the chorale phrase is again postponed. The tenors, however, begin it immediately in quick notes, and the altos embellish it with a rapid counter melody:

After the basses answer the tenor version of the phrase, the texture which grows out of the alto counter melody continues under the soprano statement:

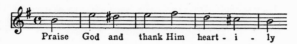

Praise God and thank Him heart - i - ly

Seventh phrase:

By the seventh phrase the music has gathered so much momentum that the long-note phrase does not appear. The tenors sing the phrase, and then it enters consecutively in the bass, alto, and soprano parts, accompanied by fragmentary echoes of the syllables of "Hallelujah."

In sing-ing Hal- le - lu - jah.

Final phrase:

"Hallelujah" ends each verse of the cantata. In the original chorale tune the music for this final phrase is simple:

Hal - le - lu -jah!

As a climax for this first verse, a climax which must carry to completion the remarkable accumulation of momentum which has preceded it, Bach builds a long passage from this simple scale which descends from dominant to tonic. He increases the speed of the music, syncopates the entrance of the scalelike subject, piles it up in imitation, and gives it a counter melody which climbs an octave in rapid notes:

The members of Bach's Easter Sunday congregation in 1724 never heard of swing, but Bach swings this "Hallelujah," and there can be no doubt that he did it for the very reason that we of the twentieth century enjoy swing. Energy accumulates to a degree where its forward motion is irrepressible, and it begins to tumble over itself to reach its goal. The musical process induces the sense of energy in the listener by its own superabundant display of energy. Reiterated syncopation, whether in the music of Bach, Beethoven, Brahms, or the twentieth century swing musicians who sometimes think they discovered it, results in a magnificent display of energy. Notice, too, the effect of massive strength which results, at the end of this verse, from the organ point on the dominant.

This first verse has been analyzed in considerable detail because it sets the pattern for the sort of thing the listener may expect in the succeeding verses. As with the Brahms symphony, the listener must expect to have this music grow on him. Listen to it many times. Its magnificent fabric—and the relationship of that fabric to the text—will become increasingly clear.

VERSE II

Death's thrall not one could hope to break
Among the children of mankind;
Our sin it was, Death's power did make,
There was no guiltless soul to find.
Therefore came Death's bitter hour
When he took o'er us the power,
Held us in his kingdom fast.
Hallelujah!

The second verse is a duet between the sopranos and altos of the chorus, with an accompaniment by the organ and the violoncello. Bach indicated that other instruments should play in unison with the voices, as he did for the first verse; but this indication is seldom followed in performance. A reading of the text for the verse will indicate that the mood has changed. Verse I started the resurrection drama at Easter. Verse II turns back momentarily to the somber background of the Easter celebration. Bach's setting has the effect of lifting the curtain on a scene of lamentation.

Notice how the short introduction slides downhill and how the bass grows out of the first two notes of the chorale melody:

The voice parts, when they enter, imitate each other with the same descending figure, the first two notes of the chorale:

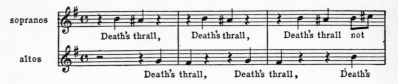

Notice the powerful downward pull of the dissonances in the setting of the "Hallelujah." We used this as an illustration in Chapter 6. There is no jubilation here!

VERSE III

Jesus Christ, God's only Son,
Came to help us in our need.
All sin's works He hath undone,
From Death's presence hath us freed.
Gone his powers and his domains
The form alone of Death remains,
And Christ has robbed Death's sting of pain.
Hallelujah!

As the text indicates, here is the happy answer to the gloom of the previous verse. Again the mood of the music changes completely, and again Bach signifies the change not by composing new music but by devising a new treatment for the tune of the chorale. The rapid accompanying figuration grows out of the first three notes of the chorale:

The upward march of the bass is calculated to add strength to the rapid motion of the upper parts:

Above this fabric the tenors of the chorus sing one phrase after another of the chorale, with rests between phrases:

Notice how effectively Bach calls attention to the word and the idea of "Death" by first transferring the rapid motion to the bass and then stopping the instrumental parts altogether while the voices hold the long note. The whole effect is increased by the sudden rush of the original speed when the vocal phrase is finished:

As an ending for this verse Bach writes another jubilant, although short, setting for the "Hallelujah." The music here grows out of the rapid accompanying fabric:

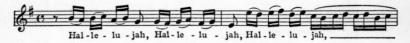

Hal-le-lu-jah, Hal-le-lu-jah, Hal-le-lu-jah,

VERSE IV

It was a wondrous war to see,
When Death and Life engaged in strife.
With Life remains the victory.
For Death is swallowed up in Life.
Scripture tells the tidings true
How one death the other slew.
And Death is made a mockery.
Hallelujah!

The war between Life and Death was "a wondrous war to see." For this verse Bach made a polyphonic fabric which is wondrous to hear. Each pair of lines of the text has a little war in which their melodic phrases take part. The tenors sing their first phrase, and as they repeat "a wondrous war to see" with a new continuing phrase, the altos answer with the second phrase. All the parts are talking at once as the fabric weaves on:

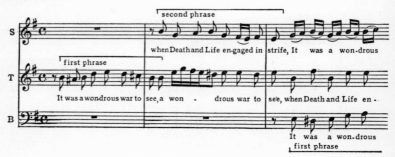

When this rapid-moving polyphonic web is well started, the altos sing, in slower notes, the first phrase and later the second phrase of the chorale tune. As the verse continues, the music of each pair of phrases receives a comparable musical setting. The excitement of the music is heightened by the device of bringing the imitation between parts closer together. For the lines beginning "For Death," "Scripture tells," and "How one death," each part follows upon the heels of the preceding in imitation which has the intensity of a canon:

The setting of the "Hallelujah" brings all four parts together. Notice the effect of tremendous vitality as the tenors punctuate the smooth motion of the other voices with their crisp, quick notes.

VERSE V

Behold our rightful paschal Lamb,
Whom God long since ordained,
Should hang upon the Cross's stem
By fires of love constrained.
Whose blood shall be upon our door
A pledge of faith, when Death goes by,
To warn him he can harm no more.
Hallelujah!

Bach has by no means exhausted the devices by which he can extract a new mood from the original chorale tune. This verse is given to the basses of the choir. The rhythm is changed from four beats in a measure to three. The accompaniment begins with a softly descending progression which again reflects the first two notes of the chorale tune. Above this a rolling eighth-note figure gives a forward motion that will continue through most of the verse:

The structure of the melodic line for this verse is interesting. Except for the one beginning "Whose blood," each line of the text is sung twice, first to the melody of the chorale and second to a free-flowing phrase of equal length. Above the free melodic phrase the orchestra answers, at a new level, with the melody that the voices have just sung. The treatment of the first line is characteristic:

As the verse continues, notice how Bach emphasizes the idea expressed in the line beginning "Whose blood" by changing momentarily to major and by extending his treatment of it. Notice, too, the wide range of the voice parts from a very low, long-held note on the word "Death" to the long, high note on the word "warn." Again there is an interesting and new treatment of the "Hallelujah."

VERSE VI

So let us keep the Easter feast
With heartfelt joy and gladness,
Since God Himself is now our Sun,
And doth dispel our sadness.

Who by His most gracious light,
Hath made our spirits pure and bright.
The night of sin has vanished.
Hallelujah!

The mood is now one of jubilation. The verse is given to
the sopranos and tenors. The accompaniment begins with a
marchlike passage in which the first three notes of the
chorale are hidden and from which the rapid motion of the
voice parts will later develop:

Notice the imitation between parts as the voices move from
one phrase of the melody to another. The long chains of
triplets with which Bach illustrates the ideas of "gladness,"
of "dispelling sadness," of "gracious light," and of "spirits
pure and bright" are memorable, and so is the long passage
on the word "vanish." The music for the "Hallelujah" grows
out of the light and rapid motion which has characterized
the whole verse, but it is at the same time related to the corresponding phrase of the original melody:

Hal -   - le -lu-jah

VERSE VII

Lo, now we eat true paschal bread
Sent down to man from Heaven,
Because the gracious God hath said,
We need not the old leaven.
Christ is now our food indeed,
On Christ alone our souls must feed,
For faith no other Life admits.
Hallelujah!

This is the final verse, the simple harmonization of the tune for which Luther originally wrote the text. We knew it before we heard the cantata. Heard at the end, it has the effect of a monumental benediction. Bach must have anticipated the effect of climax which would be given by the massive simplicity of this chorale. The six verses that precede it are, in a sense, a prelude to its magnificence.

Bach and his congregation must have felt at the close of the cantata that both composer and listeners had had a successful day. Many of the listeners, perhaps, had missed some of the intricacies of the work, but its grandeur would grow on them. And they were not unused to intricate music; their musicians served it to them often. Bach often played fugues for them on the organ, and a fugue is intricate.

What is a fugue? It is, above all, not a formula. Prospective composers have to study it as though it were a formula, but the listener may regard it simply as a vehicle which uses in characteristic patterns the devices for weaving an expressive musical texture which have been observed in the cantata. Some of the verses of the cantata approach fugue form. They all make a fugal use of the thematic material. To think about them as fugues would be a mistake from the stand-point of the listener. In all probability Bach did not think about them in that way. He was using his manner of making music to develop an expressive setting for his text.

The most characteristic aspect of the fugue texture is its beginning. Each voice—there may be from two to six—begins the subject afresh when it enters, and at a new entry of the subject each voice already sounding goes on with the counter subject. The second entry of the subject is called the answer, because it comes on a different level from the first announcement of the subject. The fact that subject and answer occur on different levels sets up for the fugue a basic pattern in which the whole fabric moves, in its middle section, to the key of the level on which the answer appeared. For its last section it moves back to the original key. The last section is marked, too, by a re-entry of the voices in an imitative procedure similar to that of the beginning.

The listener has the feeling at the beginning of a fugue that the parts of the texture are taking their places and speaking their pieces one by one.

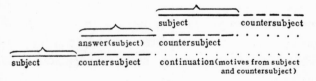

The movement of the Bach Concerto for two violins that was studied in Chapter 5 is a fugue with an accompaniment. The two solo violins enter characteristically:

subject

answer – a fifth higher than subject

countersubject

When all voices have entered, the melodic lines in the continuation grow out of the motives of the subject matter.

Music, like any other language, can be used for many purposes. We have studied music which was composed for a high purpose. We have tried to learn to perceive that purpose in our listening. In the twentieth century, great music is accessible in a physical sense to nearly everyone. In any other sense it lies open only to those who will learn its language. Such music, if the listener will but give it the opportunity, can speak to him of an ideal world where the struggles and disappointments and achievements of mankind are transmuted into another kind of reality—into eloquent fabrics of sound which lend their perfection to whatever of human striving and aspiration they express and which thus create for a moment not the illusion but the actuality of perfection.

RECORDING

Bach   Cantata No. 4, "Christ lay fast bound in Death's
            harsh chain"   Victor M-120

Appendix

MUSICAL FUNDAMENTALS

MUSICAL FUNDAMENTALS

MUSICAL SOUNDS

THE sounds that constitute the raw material out of which music is made range approximately from 28 vibrations per second to 5000. The ear can perceive slightly lower and much higher sounds—sounds which function as overtones and thus determine tone-color, but which are not directly notated for music. Thus the range of sounds notated for musical use because they can be played on musical instruments is fairly wide. Not all of the distinctly perceptible sounds within this range are usable for Western music, because no systematic relationship can be established among them. One sound—by itself—is not music, nor are many sounds if they lack perceptible relationship.

The musical experience of the Western world—Chinese and Hindu musicians are among those who have had different experience—has led to the establishment of a definite musical system within the range of sounds which has been described in terms of vibrations. This system is perceptible to all of us who have been conditioned by our participation in Western musical culture. It consists of a means of identifying sounds, an organization of sounds on the basis of scales and keys, and a means of notation.

LETTER NAMES OF SOUNDS

For the purposes of music, sounds are identified by letters. Because the whole system of musical relationships is based on the repetition of the octave, only seven letter names, the first seven letters of the alphabet, are necessary. Thus the letter A represents a series of sounds separated by octaves, for which the vibration speeds are as follows:

$$
\begin{array}{ll}
3520 & \text{(highest A)} \\
1760 & \\
880 & \\
440 & \\
220 & \\
110 & \\
55 & \\
27\frac{1}{2} & \text{(lowest A)}
\end{array}
$$

The letter C in like manner represents another series of vibrations:

$$
\begin{array}{ll}
4096 & \text{(highest C)} \\
2048 & \\
1024 & \\
512 & \\
256 & \text{(middle C)} \\
128 & \\
64 & \\
32 & \text{(lowest C)}
\end{array}
$$

It should be noticed that, beginning at the bottom of each column, the next highest number is always twice as big as the one below. In terms of vibrations, this means that the sound of any tone in the series is produced by a vibration just twice as fast as that of the next lowest tone with the same letter name. This relationship between octaves—the distance from any tone to the nearest tone with the same letter name—can be represented in terms of vibration speed by the formula 2:1. The physical properties of such closely related sounds account for the fact that our musical system is organized on the basis of octave repetition. Because of that fact we need only seven letter names.

Sounds that are related to each other in the octave relationship are not, for musical purposes, totally different sounds. A soprano and a bass singing the same melody, for instance, will hardly be conscious that they are singing an octave apart. Each will be singing sounds which have the same letter name.

THE DIATONIC SERIES

The background of the discovery of the diatonic series is obscure. Probably it was used for musical purposes before it was completely understood. Whatever its derivation, however, it furnishes patterns for the sounds within the range of each octave of our musical system. When the octave was first perceived as a musical relationship which could be expressed in terms of a mathematical formula, the discovery led to an examination, in terms of similar formulas, of other musical relationships. That examination located, within each octave, an intermediate tone which implies the whole diatonic scale pattern. The new tone within the octave had the relationship to the lower tone of the octave of 3:2. It was, in modern terminology, the fifth.

Once the relationships of the fifth and the octave were defined, the diatonic series could be produced by moving around a circle of fifths. Beginning with C (256), for instance, the process would be as follows: The fifth below C is F. The fifth above C is G. Moving up by fifths from G gives the following row: G, D, A, E, B. Making use of the octave relationship and placing the tones consecutively gives the diatonic series:

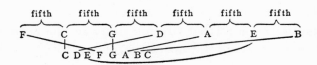

This series of tones—represented for the present by their letter names—falls into a distinct ladderlike pattern which is called diatonic. The pattern arises out of the fact that the intervals between the steps in the series are of two kinds, large and small—whole steps and half steps. The half steps fall between E and F and between B and C. All the other intervals are whole steps. A diagram of the pattern looks like a ladder, with the rungs closer together in two places than in any others:

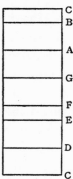

As a pattern for the diatonic series, this ladder can be used at any position in our musical system. Moving it, however, entails the use of sounds other than those represented by the simple letter names. To understand the derivation of these other sounds we must turn to a discussion of the chromatic series.

THE CHROMATIC SERIES

As musicians used the diatonic patterns, they discovered that it was necessary to locate half steps within all of the whole-step intervals. Because the letter names already had been used in their alphabetical order to describe the positions within the diatonic series, another terminology was necessary. Out of this necessity grew our rather confusing use of the sharp and flat signs. If the half step below a diatonic position is to be used as a substitute for the sound with the simple letter name, it will be known by the name of that sound with the word "flat" added. Thus when the half step below B is substituted for B, it will be called B flat. If, similarly, the half step above a diatonic position is to be substituted, it will be known by the name of that sound with the word "sharp" added. Thus if the half step above F is to be substituted for F, it will be called F sharp.

The row of tones which includes all of the half steps within the octave is called the chromatic series. Its structure can be shown by a diagram. Notice that each position not shown in the diagram of the diatonic series (and other positions too, in substitute relationships) may be known by either of two names.

```
                C                    C ····· B sharp
        C  flat ·····B               B
        B  flat ······               ······ A sharp
                A                    A
        A  flat ······      ................      ······ G sharp
                G                    G
        G  flat ······               ······ F sharp
                F                    F ····· E sharp
        F  flat ····· E              E
        E  flat ······      ................      ······ D sharp
                D                    D
        D  flat ······               ······ C sharp
                C                    C
```

It should be noted that the chromatic positions can be explained also on the basis of a continuation of the circle of fifths with which the diatonic positions were located. A continuation of the circle past seven positions produces the chromatic tones:

C flat | G flat D flat A flat E flat B flat F C G D A E B F sharp G sharp D sharp A sharp | E sharp

The picture of musical fundamentals would be complicated unnecessarily by an attempt to show why F sharp and G flat, for instance, are not absolutely identical. For all practical purposes they are; by a long-standing compromise between natural fact and practical necessity, which is called equal temperament, the octave is divided into twelve equal half-step intervals—the chromatic series.

NOTATION

Long before an understanding of musical materials had progressed to the point where the chromatic series was recognized, musicians found that the preservation and performance of their music necessitated a notation which would be

more usable than the letter names of sounds. Our notation
has developed in conjunction with expanding concepts of
our musical system; it contains some anomalies which musicians are forced to tolerate largely because of tradition.

The symbols by which music is notated consist of the following:

1. The Staff
The staff has five lines. Each line and each intervening
space represent a pitch position:

The lines and spaces of the staff have no definite meaning,
however, until a clef is placed upon the staff.

2. The Clef
The clef is always seen at the left end of the staff. Three
clefs are in common use in present-day music.

G clef (commonly called "treble" or "soprano" clef) : &

This clef locates the G above middle C by its position
on the staff.

Thus, with the G clef placed on the staff, the lines and
spaces take on definite meaning:

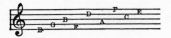

F clef (commonly called the "bass" clef) : ✸

This clef locates the F below middle C. The F line runs
between the two dots.

With the F clef placed on the staff, the lines and spaces

take on a definite meaning, a meaning which does not overlap with that of the G clef.

Music for the piano is commonly written on two staffs.
When two staffs are used, with the G clef on the upper and
the F clef on the lower, the pitch which is common to both
is notated by an added or ledger line below the upper or
above the lower staff. Ledger lines may be used at will with
any clef. They and the spaces between them will represent
a continuation up or down of the relationship established by
the clef on the staff to which they are connected.

C clef: 𝄡

The C clef locates middle C. It is used in two positions. It
is commonly called the "alto" clef when it locates middle
C on the third line of the staff:

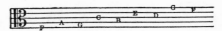

When it locates middle C on the next to the top line of the
staff it is commonly called the "tenor" clef.

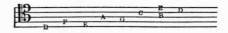

3. Notes

Individual sounds are represented by placing notes in the
desired position on the staff. Notes are used, however, not
only to locate pitch, but to indicate duration. The scale of

duration values, which are represented relatively, is as follows:

whole note	𝅝	𝅝 = 𝅗𝅥 𝅗𝅥	
half note	𝅗𝅥	𝅗𝅥 = 𝅘𝅥 𝅘𝅥	
quarter note	𝅘𝅥	𝅘𝅥 = 𝅘𝅥𝅮 𝅘𝅥𝅮 or 𝅘𝅥𝅮𝅘𝅥𝅮	
eighth note	𝅘𝅥𝅮	𝅘𝅥𝅮 = 𝅘𝅥𝅯 𝅘𝅥𝅯 or 𝅘𝅥𝅯𝅘𝅥𝅯	
sixteenth note	𝅘𝅥𝅯	𝅘𝅥𝅯 = 𝅘𝅥𝅰 𝅘𝅥𝅰 or 𝅘𝅥𝅰𝅘𝅥𝅰	
thirty-second note	𝅘𝅥𝅰	𝅘𝅥𝅰 = 𝅘𝅥𝅱 𝅘𝅥𝅱 or 𝅘𝅥𝅱𝅘𝅥𝅱	
sixty-fourth note	𝅘𝅥𝅱		

From this chart it will be seen that each note is equal in
length to two of the next shorter notes. When it is necessary
to show a division in multiples of three each note is followed
by a dot. Thus a dotted whole note is equal in duration to
three half notes; a dotted quarter note equals three eighth
notes:

$$𝅝 \cdot = 𝅗𝅥 \; 𝅗𝅥 \; 𝅗𝅥$$

$$𝅘𝅥 \cdot = 𝅘𝅥𝅮 \; 𝅘𝅥𝅮 \; 𝅘𝅥𝅮 \quad or \quad 𝅘𝅥𝅮𝅘𝅥𝅮𝅘𝅥𝅮$$

The dot has the effect, then, of lengthening by half as much
again the note which it follows. Naturally it does not cover
all of the necessities which may arise. If, for instance, it is
desired that the length of time normally allotted to a given
note be divided into three equal parts, the sign indicating
triplets must be used:

$$𝅘𝅥 = \overset{3}{\overgroup{𝅘𝅥𝅮 \; 𝅘𝅥𝅮 \; 𝅘𝅥𝅮}} \quad or \quad \overset{3}{\overgroup{𝅘𝅥 \; 𝅘𝅥𝅮}}$$

$$𝅗𝅥 = \overset{3}{\overgroup{𝅘𝅥 \; 𝅘𝅥 \; 𝅘𝅥}} \quad or \quad \overset{3}{\overgroup{𝅗𝅥 \; 𝅘𝅥}}$$

$$𝅝 = \overset{3}{\overgroup{𝅗𝅥 \; 𝅗𝅥 \; 𝅗𝅥}} \quad or \quad \overset{3}{\overgroup{𝅝 \; 𝅗𝅥}}$$

4. Rests

The entire system of notes indicating duration of sounds is duplicated in a similar system of "rests" indicating duration of silences. The system of rests may be diagrammed as follows:

whole rest	▬
half rest	▬
quarter rest	𝄽
eighth rest	𝄾
sixteenth rest	𝄿
thirty-second rest	𝅀
sixty-fourth rest	𝅁

Rests may be dotted and may be used with the sign of triplet value in exactly the same manner as notes.

5. Beat and Measure

The basic time unit in music is the beat. The forward motion of music is measured by the more or less regular recurrence of strong and weak beats. The pattern formed by the succession of strong and weak beats is the measure. Its length is determined by the number of beats it contains. Each measure is marked off by a bar line.

6. Time Signature

The time signature states the relative duration values and the length of the measure. It consists of two numbers, or a conventional sign understood to replace two numbers, at the right of the clef at the beginning of any given piece of music. If there are to be four beats in the measure and a quarter note is to receive one beat, the time signature will indicate the number of beats in the measure with the number

4 in the numerator and the kind of note to get one beat with the number 4 in the denominator:

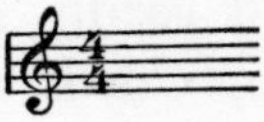

Here is a table of commonly used time signatures:

4 beats to a measure, ♩ (4) gets one beat

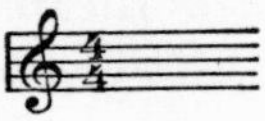 or 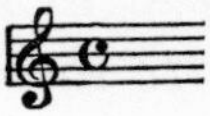

3 beats to a measure, ♩ (4) gets one beat

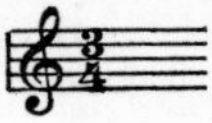

2 beats to a measure, 𝅗𝅥 (2) gets one beat

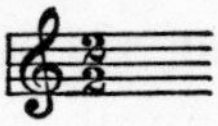 or 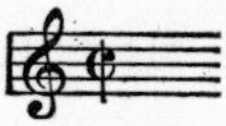

6 beats to a measure, ♪ (8) gets one beat

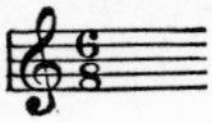

2 beats to a measure, ♩ (4) gets one beat

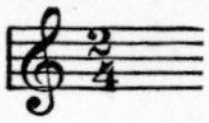

3 beats to a measure, ♪ (8) gets one beat

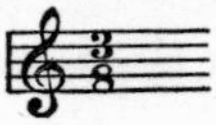

12 beats to a measure, ♪ (8) gets one beat

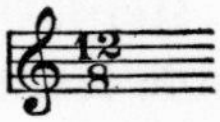

7. Indication of Speed

Two methods are used, often together, to indicate the speed at which beats will recur. The oldest method makes use of a word or group of words which have a traditionally accepted meaning. Although composers would probably prefer to use their own language, the conventional language for indicating speed of movement is Italian. Thus *largo* means very slow, *adagio* means slow, *andante* means moderately slow, *allegretto* means moderately fast, *allegro* means fast or lively, *presto* means very fast.

The second method for indicating speed is based on the use of the metronome, a clocklike device which may be adjusted to click any required number of times a minute. The metronome was invented by Maelzel. The composer uses the abbreviation for the words Maelzel Metronome (M.M.), followed by the note which gets one beat, the sign of equality, and a number which indicates the number of beats per minute. The occurrence of two beats each second, or 120 per minute, with a quarter note getting one beat, would be indicated thus: M.M. ♩=120

8. Sharps, Flats, Naturals

The use of chromatic alterations necessitates a method for their indication in notation.

To raise by one half step the pitch indicated by any note on the staff, the sharp sign ♯ is placed before it.

To lower by one half step the pitch indicated by any note on the staff, the flat sign ♭ is placed before it.

To raise by two half steps the pitch indicated by any note on the staff, the double sharp sign ✕ is placed before it.

To lower by two half steps the pitch indicated by any note on the staff, the double flat sign ♭♭ is placed before it.

To remove the effect of any sharp or flat sign, the natural sign ♮ is used.

9. Key Signature

Key signature is part of the mechanics of notation, and as such must be discussed in that connection. It will be explained at this point, however, in terms only of what already has been covered.

Key refers, fundamentally, to the position within the chromatic series of the particular seven-tone diatonic series which is to govern any given piece of music. The letter name for the sound which appears at the bottom of the diatonic pattern is the name of the key.

It will be remembered that the staff was originally conceived to notate the diatonic series in which each sound is represented by an unmodified letter name. As the sounds of the chromatic series became available and the possibility of moving the diatonic series to other pitches became apparent, the staff itself needed to be altered. This alteration was brought about by placing the necessary sharps or flats in a key signature at the immediate right of the clef on the staff.

At this point it will help to return to the diagrams of the diatonic and chromatic series.

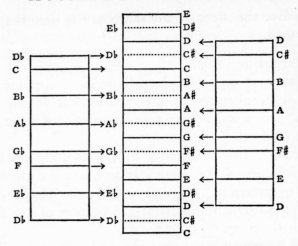

The ladder in the center represents the chromatic series, extended over more than an octave. The ladders on each side represent the diatonic series. Examine first the one at the right. With its lowest rung placed opposite D it points out the diatonic series D E F♯ G A B C♯ D. To represent a diatonic series beginning on D, then, the F line and C space on the staff (using the G clef) would have to be raised one half step. The key signature for this series on D would, in consequence, have two sharps:

The same process applies to the ladder on the left. Its bottom rung is placed opposite D♭. The ladder points out the series D♭ E♭ F G♭ A♭ B♭ C D♭. Thus the lines or spaces for D, E, G, A, B must be lowered. The key signature will contain five flats:

These diagrams have been used simply to demonstrate the source of the key signature as a part of notation. The key signature uses sharps or flats to alter the pitch meaning of the lines and spaces of the staff. That alteration continues, not only for the staff but for all ledger lines and spaces that may be added on either side of it.

SCALE AND KEY

We have been using the expression "diatonic series" in order to establish concepts which are prerequisite to the description and understanding of scale and key. A scale is a series of sounds in any pattern for which recognizable relationships can be established. The diatonic series is one very important scale pattern. The music which we ordinarily hear makes use of several scale patterns—or, more simply, scales.

1. The Major Scale

Here we meet another name for what we have been calling the diatonic series. It is the familiar *do re mi fa sol la ti do* scale, with half steps between *mi* and *fa,* the third and fourth steps of the scale, and between *ti* and *do,* the seventh and first steps of the scale.

2. The Minor Scales

It is possible, if the relationships can be established, to use any consecutive seven steps of the diatonic series as a pattern for a scale. By extending the diatonic series two octaves it will be clear that any seven-tone segment may function as a scale without alteration. Only one such segment is in common use. It begins and ends on the sixth step of the major scale, and it is the basis for all our minor scales: the *natural* minor scale. Basically it is a rearrangement of the intervals of the major scale:

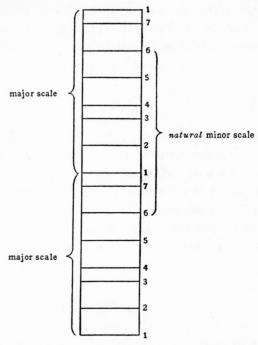

Side by side, the differences of the patterns show plainly:

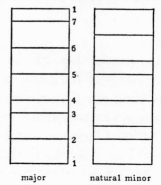

When a major scale and a minor scale are both made up of the same sounds, the difference being simply that of pattern, they are said to be related. Thus each major scale has its relative minor. If the major scale pattern covers the sounds represented by C D E F G A B C, the relative natural minor will cover the same sounds arranged in a different pattern: A B C D E F G A.

The natural minor has some characteristics which are drawbacks to its usefulness. By introducing slight changes which do not spoil its feeling of "minorness," two other types of minor have resulted. The first of these is the *harmonic* minor. For the harmonic minor scale the seventh step of the natural minor scale is raised one half step:

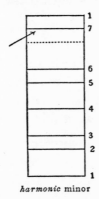

harmonic minor

The second modification of the natural minor is called the *melodic* minor. Here the scale has one pattern ascending and another descending. For the ascending scale, steps six and seven of the natural minor are raised one half step. The descending scale is the unchanged natural minor:

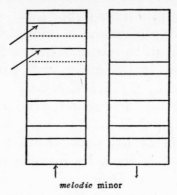

melodic minor

The major scale and the various forms of the minor scale are all considered to be diatonic patterns. As patterns they may be used at any pitch level within the chromatic series.

3. Tonality

The sounds which make up the pattern of any scale, major or minor, fall into a relationship to each other which constitutes a kind of musical solar system. Those relationships have become crystallized in a name for each scale step which describes its functional relationship to the scale as a whole:

SCALE STEP	FUNCTIONAL NAME
I	tonic
7	leading tone
6	submediant
5	dominant
4	subdominant
3	mediant
2	supertonic
I	tonic

The tonic is the end tone, the final, the governing sound of the scale. Its position defines the tonality, the level, of the scale.

The supertonic has the function which its name implies. It is immediately above the tonic, and it has a tendency, both melodic and harmonic, to point toward the tonic.

The mediant is so named because it falls halfway between the tonic and the dominant. It is a stepping stone for movement between the two.

The subdominant is the sound which dominates the scale series from five steps below the tonic. It has a strong pointing relationship to the tonic and a somewhat weaker relationship to the dominant.

The dominant governs the direction of movement within the scale from the position five steps above the tonic. Next to the tonic, it is the most important position in the scale.

The submediant is the position halfway between the tonic and the subdominant. It serves as a stepping stone between tonic and subdominant.

The leading tone points strongly to the tonic from below.

This series of relationships, only the barest outline of which is indicated by the functional names, constitutes one important aspect of key for which the word tonality is often used. Whether a scale is in major or minor mode, the sounds within it are drawn together into a strong and definite relationship by tonality.

4. Key

We have now established the fundamental characteristics of scales and tonality. Any scale, and the tonality of which it is the skeleton, may start at any of the pitch levels represented by the sounds of the chromatic series. *The level at which it is used is the key.* The key is identified by the letter name of the sound upon which the tonic occurs. Thus, if the tonic of a major scale pattern falls on C, it will be the C major scale, and the music will be in the key of C. If the

tonic of any minor scale falls on E flat, for instance, it will
be an E flat minor scale and the music will be in the key of
E flat minor.

5. Key and Key Signature

Key signature has been discussed as a means of changing
the pitch meaning of the positions on the staff. It is obvious
that such changes are made in order to match the pitch
meaning of the staff positions with the key of the music.
The fact that the key may be either major or minor has an
important implication with regard to key signature. Because
the diatonic series may be used in either a major or a minor
pattern, every key signature will fit two keys, the major and
its relative minor. An illustration will make this clear:

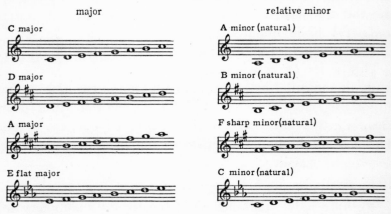

One other point should be mentioned in this connection.
A major key and a minor key on the same level—that is,
having the same letter name—will have different key signatures. Major and minor keys which have the same tonic are
said to have a tonic relationship:

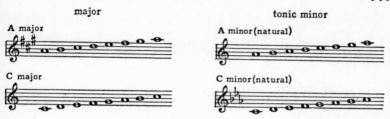

major   tonic minor

A major   A minor (natural)

C major   C minor (natural)

HARMONY

1. Intervals

An interval is the distance between two sounds, whether they are heard consecutively or simultaneously. Our discussion will be limited to the simultaneous relationship.

Intervals are measured by counting the distance in scale steps from the lower to the upper sound of the interval in terms of the major scale of which the lower sound would be tonic. The interval will have, first, a numerical name. If the bottom sound is C and the top sound A, the interval will be a sixth:

Theoretically, intervals may be given any numerical name that does not exceed the pitch range of musical sounds; practically they may be unisons, seconds, thirds, fourths, fifths, sixths, sevenths, octaves, ninths, tenths, elevenths, etc.

Because of the differences between the major and minor patterns and because, too, of the possibilities of chromatic alteration, a numerical name is not enough to complete the identification of an interval. There may be, for example, several different sizes of thirds or sixths. The size of the intervals between the tonic and the succeeding scale steps in the major scale are taken as the norm:

unison,   second,   third,   fourth,   fifth,   sixth,   seventh,   octave
perfect   *major*   *major*   *perfect*   *perfect*   *major*   *major*   *perfect*

A major interval made smaller by one half step becomes a minor interval:

major sixth   minor sixth

A minor interval made larger by one half step becomes a major interval:

minor third   major third

A perfect interval or a minor interval, made smaller by one half step, becomes a diminished interval:

perfect fifth   diminished fifth

minor seventh   diminished seventh

A perfect interval or a major interval, made larger by one half step, becomes an augmented interval:

perfect fifth   augmented fifth

major third   augmented third

2. Interval Inversion

An interval may be inverted in two ways. The lower sound may be placed an octave higher, or the upper sound may be placed an octave lower:

By inversion, unisons become octaves;
            seconds become sevenths;
            thirds become sixths;
            fourths become fifths;
            fifths become fourths;
            sixths become thirds;
            sevenths become seconds;
            octaves become unisons.

By inversion, major intervals become minor;
            minor intervals become major;
            augmented intervals become diminished;
            diminished intervals become augmented;
            perfect intervals remain perfect (hence the use
                of the word "perfect" in the nomencla-
                ture).

3. Triads

The simplest complete chord consists of three sounds, a
root, a third, and a fifth:

The seven triads belonging to any key are built on the
seven scale steps of that key. Each triad has one of the scale
steps as its root and consists of that root with the third and
the fifth above it. Each triad gets its name from the functional name of the scale step which is its root. In minor the
scale steps of the harmonic minor are the root tones for the
triads.

The triads which appear normally in major and minor fall into four classes: major, minor, diminished, augmented.

A major triad is composed of root, *major third*, perfect fifth. The triads on the tonic, dominant, and subdominant in major, and on the dominant and submediant in minor, are major triads.

A minor triad is composed of root, *minor third*, perfect fifth. The triads on the supertonic, mediant, and submediant in major, and on the tonic and subdominant in minor, are minor triads.

A diminished triad is composed of root, minor third, *diminished fifth*. The triad on the leading tone in major, and the triads on the supertonic and leading tone in minor, are diminished triads.

An augmented triad is composed of root, major third, *augmented fifth*. The triad on the mediant in minor is an augmented triad.

Triads are used as the basis for four-tone chords by using one of the tones of the triad again in the octave relationship. This device is called doubling. Usually the root of the triad is doubled:

4. Triad Inversion

The intervals within triads may be inverted without causing the triad to lose its identity. The root of the triad remains its root even when, in an inversion, it is not the lowest sound. Thus a triad on any step of the scale retains its functional identity when it is inverted.

Two inversions of triads are possible. The first inversion is the form of the triad in which the third is the lowest sound. The second inversion has the fifth at the bottom:

root position   first inversion   second inversion

5. Chords of the Seventh

It is possible to build a chord of the seventh on any scale step. The chord is composed of the root, third, fifth, and seventh. The seventh chords most commonly heard are those on the dominant and leading tone in both major and minor.

Seventh chords are susceptible to inversion. Because they have one more tone than triads they have one more inversion.

6. Altered Chords

Triads and seventh chords may be altered chromatically as the composer desires. Altered chords are usually considered to be substitutes for the chord which would normally appear in the diatonic position of the altered chord.

INDEX

accumulation of musical materials, 95-100
acoustics, 25
active harmony, 71-72
Adams, Henry, quoted, 163
allemande, 231
altered chords, 343
American Jazz Music, Hobson, quotation from, 56-57
appreciation, definition of, 3, 4
art song, 226-227
associations, power of music to make, 172-73
"Atlas" (Schubert), 227
augmented intervals, 340
augmented triad, 342

Bach, 229-32; "Brandenburg" Concerto, 231; Cantata No. 4, 73-74, 295-313; Chaconne for solo violin, 232; Concerto for two violins, 60-62, 314-15; concertos, 230-31; "Crucifixus" from Mass in B minor, 232; fugues, 230; "Goldberg" Variations, 232; Passacaglia in C minor, 232; piano music, 228; Prelude and Fugue, 98; Sinfonia, Cantata No. 4, 73-74, 295-313; violin music, 228; *Well-Tempered Clavichord,* 230
bass clarinet, 14, 18
bass drum, 15, 22
bassoon, 14, 18; double or contra, 14, 19
bass trombone, 15, 21

bass viol, 15, 25
beat, 328
Beethoven: chamber music, 229; *Coriolan* overture, 225; *Egmont* overture, 225; *Fidelio* overture, 225; *Leonora* overtures, 225; "Sonata Pathétique," 122-125; orchestra, 99; piano music, 228; Seventh Symphony, 99-100; symphonies, 219; Symphony No. 1 in C major, Op. 21, 191-213
"Bella figlia dell'amore," *Rigoletto* (Verdi), 57-59
bells, orchestral, 23
Berlioz, Hector, 220-21, 224; use of "fixed idea," 221; use of "Dies Irae," 221; "Fantastic" Symphony, 220-21
bolero, 36
bourée, 231
Brahms: chamber music, 229; comparison with Tchaikovsky, 294; First Symphony, 272-94; piano music, 228; songs, 227; symphonies, 222
"Brandenburg" Concertos (Bach), 231
brasses, 13, 19-22
bridge passage, 120; in sonata form, 145
Bruckner, symphonies, 223
Byrd, 98

Cantata No. 4, "Christ lay fast bound in Death's harsh chain" (Bach), 73-74, 295-313

passacaglia, 231; in C minor (Bach), 232
pavane, 231
percussion, 13, 22-24
perfect intervals, 340
phrase, 107
piano, 15, 23-24
piano and violin sonatas, 228
piano and violoncello sonatas, 228
Piano Concerto in A minor (Schumann), 221-22
piano: music for, 228, 229; Bach, Beethoven, Brahms, Chopin, Haydn, Liszt, Mozart, Schubert, 228; Schumann, 221-22, 228; quartet, 229; quintet, 229; sonatas by Beethoven, Haydn, Mozart, 228; trio, 229
piccolo, 14, 16
plain song, Hymn to St. John the Baptist, 97
polonaise, 36
polyphonic forms, 230; polyphonic music: Cantata No. 4 (Bach), 295-313; concerto, 230; polyphonic style, 97-98; polyphonic texture, 54-62
Pratt, Carroll C., quoted on the relation of emotion to musical value, 176-77
Prelude and Fugue (Bach), 98
preludes (Wagner): Lohengrin, 225; Meistersinger, Die, 225; Parsifal, 225; Tristan and Isolda, 28, 47-51, 225
"Prize Song," Die Meistersinger (Wagner), 103
program music: defined, 221; "Les Préludes" (Liszt), 237-42; "Don Juan" (Strauss), 242-52

quartet: "Bella figlia dell'amore," Rigoletto (Verdi), 57-59; piano, 229; string, 229

Quintet in G minor (K.V. 516), Mozart: first movement, 181-86; fourth movement, 187-90; third movement, 187-90
quintet: piano, 229; string, 229
quodlibet, 55-56

rattle, 23
recapitulation: sonata form, 145, 147-48
recording, possibilities of tone-color in, 26
reeds, 13-19
rest harmony, 71-72
rests, 328
Rhinegold, The (Wagner), 255
rhythm, 8, 31-38, 35-37
rhythmic patterns, 35-37
rhythms, dance, 35-37
Rienzi overture (Wagner), 225
Rigoletto (Verdi): "La donna è mobile," 41-45; quartet, "Bella figlia dell'amore," 57-59
Rimsky-Korsakov, "Scheherazade," 27, 226
Ring of the Nibelungen, The (Wagner), 255-56
"Rite of Spring" (Stravinsky), 99-100
rondo, 115-26; Entr'acte from Rosamunde (Schubert), 116-20, 231; form, 115; "Gipsy Rondo" (Haydn), 120-22; "Sonata Pathétique" (Beethoven), 123
root tone, 341-43
Rosamunde, Entr'acte (Schubert), 116-20
round, 54-56

"Sacre du Printemps" (Stravinsky), 99-100
sarabande, 231
saxophone, 19